Stress Management and Lo...

Acknowledgements:

I would like to thank the women and men who have, as research participants, shared their stories with me. They have enriched my work and my life. I would also like to thank my employer, West Chester University, and my department chair Loretta Rieser-Danner for her support over the years. I would, of course, not be able to complete any project without the support of my family and friends. I especially want to express my gratitude to Paul for his on-going patience and help with my various endeavors, both personal and professional.

STRESS MANAGEMENT AND LONGEVITY

The Importance of Physical and Social Activity in Later Life

Jasmin Tahmaseb McConatha, Ph.D.

Meyer & Meyer Sport

British Library Cataloguing in Publication Data
A catalogue record for this book is available from British Library

Jasmin Tahmaseb McConatha:
Stress Management and Longevity
Maidenhead: Meyer & Meyer Sport (UK) Ltd., 2014
ISBN: 978-1-78255-031-0

© 2014 by Meyer & Meyer Verlag, Aachen
Auckland, Beirut, Budapest, Cairo, Cape Town, Dubai, Indianapolis,
Kindberg, Maidenhead, Sydney, Olten, Singapore, Tehran, Toronto
Member of the World
Sport Publishers' Association (WSPA)
www.w-s-p-a.org
Printing by: B.O.S.S Druck und Medien GmbH
ISBN 978-1-78255-031-0
E-Mail: info@m-m-sports.com
www.m-m-sports.com

TABLE OF CONTENTS

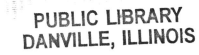

INTRODUCTION

INTRODUCTION

This book addresses the relationship between aging and stress. Research and practical suggestions emphasizing the healing power of nature, spirituality, relationships, and physical and social activity are emphasized. This book provides theories, research, and practical solutions for coping with stressful life events and changes associated with aging.

Everyone experiences stress. In fact 80% of modern diseases are linked to stress. We experience stress on a daily basis at work, at home, in traffic and noise, and regarding pollution, health concerns, and problems with relationships and family. Stress is a normal part of life. It can motivate us to work toward our goals. It can also make us aware that something is not as it should be. Being aware of stress-inducing events and how we react to them is an important ingredient in the recipe for happiness — even survival.

High levels of stress are associated with both physical and psychological problems. Each person experiences stress differently; there are even age-related changes that can lead to stress. There are also later-life transitions that are stressful.

Clearly too much stress or a person's inability to cope with it can lead to significant decline, even death. When we experience a stressful event, our bodies shift into a heightened response mode called "fight or flight." Our nervous system releases stress hormones — adrenaline and cortisol — that prepare the body for an emergency. Our heart rate increases, our muscles tighten, our blood pressure spikes, and our breath quickens. These changes can increase our physical capacities, allow us to better focus on the problem at hand, or help us flee. If they continue, they can also exhaust us and quickly deplete our physical and emotional resources leading to illness and even death.

Scientists have identified a direct link between stress and accelerated aging. They have found that intense, long-term stress can lead to an increase in the body's deterioration, reduced immune functioning, and accelerated aging. Stress can result from important life events or from routine day-to-day hassles. Everyone feels overwhelmed by actual and imagined events in the world. Positive life experiences cause stress, but it is the negative ones that are the most damaging. As the world becomes more complex, learning how to manage stress in a healthy way becomes critical to health and happiness.

AGING AND STRESS: A BRIEF OVERVIEW

The world is aging. Age is accompanied by opportunities as well as challenges. When we age, we gain wisdom and maturity. We learn that with time we can overcome problems and deal with unhappy periods in our lives. We understand that if we manage our stressful periods, they tend to pass and we can be happy again. However too many life changes or everyday hassles can lead to feeling overwhelmed and exhausted. This state can threaten our health, undermine relationships, compromise our work, and destroy our happiness.

Later life is a complex time of activity, happiness, reflection, struggle, as well as an appreciation of wisdom and insight gained from life experiences. According to lifespan developmental theorists, older men and women may experience an invigorated purpose in life, focusing remaining energies on being productive, creative, and engaging in activities and relationships that can lead to emotional satisfaction (Ryff, 1989). At the same time, older men and women are better able to avoid activities and relationship that they find unsatisfying. Later adulthood is also a time of life when we experience unavoidable losses and physical changes that may lead to stress, unhappiness, and dissatisfaction. How well we are able to cope with age related changes is a key component of maintaining well-being in later life.

PHYSICAL CHANGES AND AGE

Aging is accompanied by a certain amount of physical change. Physical declines become more noticeable. There are many slow, imperceptible changes, for example, a loss of neurons, lowered activity in the autonomic nervous system, hearing and visual impairments, weakening odor and taste sensitivity (Berk, 2010). As the body ages, a certain amount of physical decline is inevitable, however lifestyle factors, such as physical and social activity, can slow age-related decline.

AGE RELATED CHANGES CAN BE PRIMARY OR SECONDARY

1. Primary Aging: A gradual change, a slow decline; these changes are inevitable and universal.
2. Secondary Aging: Secondary changes are related to stress or illness. They result in a more dramatic deterioration due to damaging forces.
3. Tertiary aging: Changes that occur at the very end of life.

Although most elders are reasonably healthy and report high life satisfaction, there is an unavoidable increase in vulnerability to chronic illnesses as we age. Statistics indicate that eighty-five percent of those over the age of 65 have at least one chronic illness. The leading chronic conditions from which older men and women suffer include:

1. Heart disease
2. Various cancers
3. Hypertension
4. Arthritis
5. Diabetes

THE HUMAN BODY IS A MACHINE!!!

Like any machine, the system wears down. But also like any machine, how well one cares for the body influences the level of deterioration. People reach their physical peak in their 20s; beyond this point, maintenance and repair are crucial for good working order.

POSSIBLE AGE-RELATED CHANGES

1. Poor circulation
2. Cardiac arrhythmia — irregular heartbeats, very rapid and often related to salt and other minerals.
3. Angina — reduction of blood flow; supply of oxygen becomes insufficient. Chest pain is produced by exertion.
4. Myocardial interaction — most dramatic; heart attack; high mortality; coronary blood drops below necessary level, caused by spasm build-up.
5. Atherosclerosis — calcification of the arterial walls.

The above symptoms are associated with heart disease, which is the number-one killer around the world. Studies have found that heart disease is related to stress. Stress also plays a key role in hypertension or high blood pressure. Blood pressure is a dangerous illness because it has no clear symptoms, although it is related to lifestyle factors such as diet and exercise, and of course weight gain. Some statistics indicate that 35% of Americans suffer from hypertension.

Respiratory diseases are a leading cause of death in the United States and elsewhere. Respiratory diseases include asthma and emphysema. These illnesses may lead to pneumonia. They are usually treatable but can be fatal. These illnesses are related to stress, lack of exercise and, of course, smoking. Global warming and increasing pollution increase vulnerability to respiratory concerns, especially among older adults. Awareness, education, and a healthy lifestyle can moderate potentially damaging effects associated with a large percentage of respiratory problems.

Physical changes can also result in age-related stress. Changes can occur in vision. Around age 40, people begin to need reading glasses; it becomes more difficult to adjust to light changes. If one walks into a theatre, for example, it takes longer for the eyes to adjust to the dark. This can cause stress at night when older men and women drive, travel, or simply wake up and need to use the restroom.

Hearing damage also occurs. Hearing loss can result in the need for a hearing aid. Further compounding this issue, studies have found that many older men and women have self-image concerns associated with wearing a hearing aid. Hearing problems can reduce life pleasures such as listening to music and the sounds of nature. They can also negatively impact relationships. One in four people over 45 has some hearing problems. Damage occurs to the auditory system, which means ear control and sound waves function less efficiently. Hearing loss is one of the most common conditions affecting older adults. Approximately 17 percent — 36 million — of American adults report some degree of hearing loss. Men are at higher risk for hearing loss than women ("What is hearing loss?", n.d.).

Changes also can occur in taste, which makes eating less pleasurable. Physical changes in appearance are often the most dramatic and difficult to handle as they influence self-image, perceived attractiveness, and satisfaction with life. Physical changes are numerous; including but not limited to, wrinkles, changes in hair, weight, muscle tone. Skin becomes less elastic and more lined and wrinkled and drier than before. Hair gradually thins, and the amount of gray increases. Even height changes can occur so much so that older men and women can lose from 1 to 2 inches. All of the above changes are dependent upon the intersecting influences of biology, life style, and stress.

Aging is not a disease, it is influenced by:
1. Outlook/attitude
2. Social involvement
3. Physical activity and fitness
4. Inherited characteristics
5. Stress and stress management skills
6. Lifestyle
7. A spiritual orientation

Everyone has the potential to live to be 100.

An important social theory proposed by Paul Baltes (1987) focuses on the importance of making healthy adaptive choices, especially in later life. This theory, called Selective Optimization and Compensation Theory, is useful for managing the stresses of later life. According to Baltes, we cannot do everything we wish to do in life. We should focus our energies on what is important and meaningful to us and work hard at attaining important goals. It is also important to rely on external support; no one can do everything by himself.

THE IMPORTANCE OF A HEALTHY LIFESTYLE

Perhaps the most important way of managing our stress is to develop an overall healthy lifestyle. It is never too late to begin to exercise, spend time in nature, do yoga, mediate, or engage in other healthy behaviors. Health promotion is crucial and includes exercise, diet, physical and social engagement. Our goals should not be the absence of disease but the presence of optimal health and happiness.

The health promotion model (this is a holistic view of the person focusing on physical health, spirituality, psychological health, and social health) is a useful tool for gauging one's goals. At one end of the continuum is optimal well-being, happiness, and life satisfaction; at the other is disease and death. Most people strive for the middle of this continuum, where they experience no pain, where they are not anxious or depressed. In order to fully live life, it is important to create life goals that move us toward the positive end of the continuum by effectively managing life stress, engaging with nature, taking time out, having positive relationships, and enjoying life's moments.

Optimal health and well-being   Disease and death

SOCIO-EMOTIONAL SELECTIVITY THEORY

This theory can be useful in helping older men and women move toward optimal well-being. By focusing on emotion, Carstensen, Fung, & Charles (2003) explain the way older men and women feel about time left in life and how one can best make use of that time. As we age, we realize that we have limited time left — how can we most enjoy that time? How can we be productive, healthy, and happy?

What changes are necessary? How can we live in the moment? Later life is a crucial time for evaluation. We should evaluate how we spend our time, how we manage our stress, the satisfaction or lack of satisfaction we receive from our relationships. It is important to review, evaluate and make conscious choices about the time we have left.

How can we best make use of the wisdom we have gained? Research shows that as we age we are better able to manage our emotions. On a day-to-day basis older adults state experiencing low levels of anger (Tahmaseb-McConatha, Leone, & Armstrong, 1997). Contrary to negative stereotypes, elders also do not feel express negative emotion; they appear to have better inner control of those emotions. They tend to be more efficient at separating positive and negative by optimizing the positives.

GOALS OF THIS BOOK

In this book, I present an overview of the relationship between aging and effective stress management strategies. I also discuss common later life transitions that cause stress and ways older men and women can effectively cope with the stressors associated with these life changes. The book presents case study examples and practical suggestions for effective coping; suggestions that have been proven to mediate the potentially dangerous negative consequences of stress.

Chapter 1: Daily Stressors and Major Life Event Stressors — This chapter will present the reader with examples of macro-stressors, major stressful life events. I will discuss case examples of older adults who face losses, health concerns, forced retirement, and financial worries. I also present a set of effective stress management techniques that can mediate the potentially negative consequences associated with these dramatic life stressors. It is not possible to eliminate these stressors from one's life, but stress management techniques such as time management, relaxation, meditation, and mindfulness can help prevent these stressors from becoming overwhelming and destructive.

Chapter 2: Time of Our Lives — In our wired world, most people spend their time multi-tasking — rushing from place to place, answering emails and texts. There are very few moments in life in which we are not bombarded with technological demands. The itch to respond to these demands has accelerated the already fast pace of life. These days free time is a rare commodity. It is a rare moment indeed when we can do exactly what we want or spend time in a purposeful lack of activity. Increasingly, Americans are engaged in long hours of arduous work. Most Americans take very few holidays. When they do take time off, they often take their work with them thereby defeating the purpose of "time off." Even during retirement, men and women often have difficulty relaxing and engaging in leisure. This chapter discusses the health benefits of time off.

Chapter 3: Coping with Retirement: Work and retirement are very important in people's lives. Occupations shape identity and lifestyle. The average age of the workforce has increased. Ageism in the workplace has also increased. Prejudice and discrimination in the workplace can lead to feelings of worthlessness, anxiety and depression. These can result in earlier and unplanned retirement. Retirement can be a happy time for most people. It can also be a time of stress and loss, especially if it is unplanned or unwanted.

In the United States, one quarter of workers between the ages of 58 to 73 continue to work. Many older workers are worried about finances, health insurance, and the cost of living. Approximately 40% of Americans are forced into retirement for reasons beyond their control — layoffs, downsizing, and illness. Unexpected or unplanned events, such as forced early retirement can prove to be extremely stressful. Life events, such as retirement, have both positive and negative consequences. This chapter will address some of the concerns older workers face, as well as providing strategies for managing work related stress and ageism.

Chapter 4: Relationships, Social Support, and Coping with Stress — Relationships are an important source of satisfaction and support throughout life. Later adulthood presents unique challenges for the development and maintenance of satisfying relationships. In this chapter, I discuss theories and research related to some of the ways that relationships and social support can help older women and men manage and cope with later life stress. Later life can be a satisfying and connected time of life; unfortunately, studies indicate that it can also be a time of loneliness and isolation. Relationships are dynamic; as people's life circumstances and needs change so do their relationships. The one constant is that people always need other people. They need friends, family, and a community of support. Some people only need one or two people while others may need a larger network. There is no correct number as long as one is satisfied and has support during difficult times. This chapter addresses research focusing on relationship between stress, happiness, health, and relationships.

Chapter 5: Coping with Loss, Death, and Mourning — Loss is unavoidable. Everyone experiences loss. In later life, losses become more common. Coping with any loss is difficult and stressful; coping with the death of someone close to us can be overwhelming. Grieving and mourning is, of course, a deeply personal, familial and cultural experience. Everyone mourns differently. The way we mourn is shaped by our beliefs and culture. Social scientists have tried to provide help by understanding the mourning process. This chapter addresses the processes of coping with the loss of a loved one.

Chapter 6: Laugh and Pray — There are many other effective ways of coping with later life stress. According to studies, two of the most beneficial ways to cope with death are through the use of humor in difficult times and by relying on spirituality as a coping mechanism.

Humor has been known to promote positive mental health. Laughter clearly has therapeutic properties. Everyone knows that they feel better when he or she laughs. In fact, research has supported the therapeutic value of humor as a coping mechanism, a source of tension relief, and even as a mechanism of survival.

Humor also has a positive physiological impact. Historically, humor has been used a valuable tool to promote mental health. During psychotherapy, clinicians often rely upon humor. This chapter focuses on ways that humor can be used positively and productively as a coping strategy.

Spirituality is another important source of support and serves as a crucial coping mechanism during difficult times. Spirituality can take the form of religion, meditation, and communing with nature; it is a completely subjective phenomenon, which varies by individual. Regardless of the form it takes, it provides inspiration, meaning and purpose in life. It leads to a feeling of connectedness with others and with history, culture, the divine, nature, and art (Berk, 2010). This chapter discusses some of the ways that a sense of spirituality aids in coping with stress and promotes health and happiness.

Chapter 7: The Healing Power of Nature – Many of us spend our days in offices, under artificial lights, working on computers, frequently in cubicles that have no windows. When we finally complete our workday and emerge, it is often dark and we have no notion of the sunlight, woods, beaches, or even parks. Nature deprivation negatively impacts the health and happiness of people of all ages. Psychologists associate depression, anxiety, and stress with our increasing alienation from nature. This chapter focuses on the health promoting aspects of time spent in nature, the importance of paying attention to ourselves, and being mindful of how we spend our days.

We are often not aware or even psychologically present in our life experiences. We often eat, talk, drive, walk, and even have sex without fully experiencing the moment. We frequently lose awareness of what is going on in our lives. In our complex and technologically saturated world, mindlessness is becoming more and more common. We tend to multitask, simultaneously checking text messages, emails as we talk on the phone, and listen to music. As a consequence, we often do not fully attend to any of the things we are doing. Mindfulness can increase pleasure in day-to-day activities and promote well-being. This chapter presents a brief overview of mindfulness and information on increasing mindfulness.

REFERENCES

+ Baltes, P. (1987). Theoretical propositions of lifespan developmental psychology: On the dynamics between growth and decline. *Developmental Psychology*, 23(5), 611-626.

+ Berk, L. (2010). *Exploring Lifespan Development*. Boston, MA: Allyn & Bacon.

+ Carstensen, L., Fung, H., & Charles, S. (2003). Socio-emotional selectivity theory and the regulation of emotion in the second half in life. *Motivation and Emotion 27*(2), 103-123.

+ Tahmaseb-McConatha, J., Leone, F.M., & Armstrong, J.M. (1997). Emotional control in adulthood. *Psychological Reports, 80*, 499-507.

+ Ryff, C. (1989). Happiness is everything, or is it? Explorations on the meaning of psychological well-being. *Journal of Personality and Social Psychology 57*(6): 1069-1081.

+ "What is hearing loss?". (n.d.). *NIH Senior Health*. Retrieved October 15, 2013 from http://nihseniorhealth.gov/hearingloss/hearinglossdefined/01.html

CHAPTER ONE

Daily Hassles and Major Life Event Stressors

CHAPTER ONE

Daily Hassles and Major Life Event Stressors

It is four in the afternoon, and I am trying to write the first chapter of a book that focuses on the stressors of later life. In a few hours, I'll host a birthday party for my friend Peter. Nine people are coming for drinks, kabobs, rice, and birthday cake. Having grown up in a large family in which an evening meal never consisted of fewer than 10 people, the thought of preparing an 11-person dinner is not stressful. Such a situation, however, would put my otherwise very accomplished friend in a complete state of panic. Rosie is able to easily write an essay on any number of topics without feeling overwhelmed or panicked. Cooking a meal for 10, on the other hand, would stress Rosie out for a week. As for me, I have been staring at one introductory page for two days.

The situations that trigger stress vary for each of us. The differences are a result of a mysterious mix of life circumstance, experience, age, gender, personality (introversion or extroversion for example), culture, and a host of other unknown factors. Given its complexity, stress is difficult to understand and define. Clearly what is stressful for one person will not necessarily be stressful for another. Even so, there are commonalities in stress that we can associate with life circumstances. Study after study tells us that money, social relationships, work, and health concerns are common stressors among people of all ages. Later life, of course, brings its own set of stressors: declining health and energy, the impact of retirement, the loss of loved ones, evidence of bodily change, existential concerns about past accomplishments, and anxiety about future plans and options. This book addresses common stressors of later life, useful coping mechanism, and sources of support. Throughout the book, I address the importance of the healing power of positive relationships, the importance of physical and social activity, and time-off or downtime, and the benefits of spending time in nature.

If later adulthood stressors can appear overwhelming, there is some comfort in the results of gerontological research, which tells us that as we age we become better able to manage stress. With age we gain wisdom and perspective and are able to focus our energies on what we can change and manage, and we distance

ourselves from what is out of our control. Even with these improved stress management skills, stress clearly affects us in later life. What is its physical and psychological impact? What sorts of strategies are helpful for managing stress? This book addresses some stressors of the transitions and support systems in later life.

WHAT IS STRESS?

The American Institute for Stress relies on an old definition of stress first introduced by researcher Hans Selye. In the 1930s, Hans Selye defined stress as the response of the body to any demand from the environment. More common definitions consider stress a mental, physical, emotional, and behavioral reaction to any perceived demands or threats in our environment. A useful way of understanding stress is to view it as something in life that needs to be taken care of, managed, fixed, repressed, or addressed.

Almost anything can cause stress. Most of our stressors occur on a day-to-day basis: traffic; meals require preparation; bills need to be paid; errands need to be run; phone calls and emails need to be dealt with or returned. If these matters pile up, they can create considerable stress. Even if we are able to manage these day-to-day demands occasionally, in everyone's life, there is a major life event that may elicit considerable stress.

The key to managing stress is to increase our coping skills and expand our resources. In this way we are likely to avoid the worst case scenario – feeling overwhelmed by stress. We experience stress every day. It affects us as we wait for an appointment, sit in traffic, try to clean our homes, manage a meeting, and teach a class. Sometimes these everyday stresses can be overwhelming. Major stressful events can transform our lives positively and negatively. We may need to confront a serious illness. We may choose or be forced to a move to a new home. We may lose a job. We may have a loved one pass away. These major life events can be devastating. During these difficult times, how do we go on? Unfortunately, sad events are experienced by everyone. Somehow we must manage and continue living.

Everyone experiences stress throughout his or her life. Stress results from daily hassles and from significant life transitions. This chapter addresses how to cope with common day-to-day stressors such as traffic, noise, disagreeable people, household chores, and so forth. This chapter also suggests ways of viewing and managing the major life event stressors of later life. How we deal with stress is related to the balance of leisure and work, the demands generated by place and space, the joys and concerns of retirement, our personal and social resources, and our optimism, resilience, and overall well-being.

DAILY HASSLES AND MAJOR LIFE EVENTS

Researchers have divided the stressors that people experience into two categories: daily hassles and major life events. Both of these precipitate stress. The vast majority of stressors develop from daily occurrences: losing keys, sitting in traffic, running errands, being late, missing a meeting, and so forth.

Any one of these, of course, is not as important as a major life event, such as marriage, illness, or retirement. However, depending on our perception, personality, and coping abilities, everyday stressors can be just as devastating as major life changes. It is often the everyday stressors, the daily hassles, rather than the major life events, that have the most negative effect on people. After all, major life events do not occur regularly, but we experience hassles each and every day. In short, day-to-day hassles can wear us down more than infrequently occurring major life events.

For their part, major life events can be expected or unexpected. Everyone is aware of the possibility that one's life can change in an instant. One day we are happily cooking a meal or taking a walk. Twenty-four hours later our life has changed dramatically as we suddenly find ourselves faced with unexpected and stressful circumstances with which we must come to terms. Thankfully such events tend not to occur too frequently. Unexpected major life events, which are usually unpleasant, are much more stressful than anticipated and planned ones.

Regardless of the state of planning and expectation, major life events cause considerable stress and require adjustments and adaptation. Almost 50 years ago, Holmes and Rahe (1967) developed a measure of stressful life events. They call it the Social Readjustment Rating Scale (SRRS) or the Holmes and Rahe Stress Scale. This instrument is still one of the most useful tools for measuring stress. Holmes and Rahe considered how stress is linked to illness by asking medical patients about the major events they had experienced in the past two years. Equipped with these answers, Holmes and Rahe produced a list of 43 stressful life events.

Holmes and Rahe then gave each of the events a weight based on how stressful they were likely to be. Examples include serious life changes, such as the death of a spouse (100 points) or going through a divorce (73 points) to more pleasurable, less serious events such as taking a vacation (13 points) or changing one's social habits (18 points). The more stressful events a person experiences, the more likely he or she is to become vulnerable to illness. Those scoring 300 or more points are at a high risk for becoming ill; those scoring 150 to 299 points are considered to be at a moderate risk. Respondents who score below 150 points have the least vulnerability to illness. The complete instrument can be located online.

Instruments such as the Holmes and Rahe Social Readjustment Rating Scale can increase our awareness of the stressors in our lives and of the need to take action. Becoming aware of the possible impact of life events is important, but of course each person will react differently to a specific event. The Holmes and Rahe scale is a very useful tool to assess the amount of stress we experience in a given year. It also pinpoints who may be vulnerable to illness. In such cases, professionals may suggest that those scoring high on the scale may need to take some proactive measures and increase their stress management skills.

WHY IS MY HEART RACING?

People perceive stress differently and experience differing physical and psychological reactions to it. Many factors play a role in what we perceive as stressful and how we respond to stress. These factors are individual, situational, and culturally conditioned. Cultural expectations play an important role in determining what we find stressful. Cultural messages influence our expectations for ourselves. If we are not measuring up to standards, we can feel anxious and stressed.

We have learned that the best way to maintain our physical and psychological abilities is to use them. Contemporary models of aging encourage elders to remain physically and socially active. Messages relating to activity tend to actually promote well-being, but they can also lead to frustration and anxiety.

The cases of Simine and Karen illustrate how individual differences can lead to different expectations of everyday activities and varying expectations about how to remain active. As we will see, one person's well-being can be bolstered by physical and social activity, while the demands of the same activity can hinder another person.

Simine and Karen are friends. They have lived in similar houses in the same neighborhood for more than 20 years. They are both in their 60s; they are healthy as well as being physically and socially active. They have large families with brothers, sisters, children, and grandchildren. They also have a large network of friends who often come to visit them or invite them to weekend gatherings at their country houses.

Simine is happy with her daily plans, chores, and activities. She loves having company, likes to cook for large groups of people, and enjoys travel. If she's busy, she's happy. Karen, on the other hand, used to enjoy the swirl of social activity but finds that it is now becoming too much for her. Although she loves her family and friends, she finds it increasingly difficult to keep up with all of their activities and concerns. She also finds it difficult to manage household chores.

Simine and Karen present good examples of the impact of personality and age on perceptions of stress. As Simine ages, she is happy to continue the activity patterns she established years ago. She is an extroverted high-energy person who thrives on activity. Karen, by contrast, now feels tired and overwhelmed. In order to maintain her happiness, she recognizes that she needs to make some changes.

Twenty years ago, psychologist Laura Carstensen (1993) introduced a theory of Social and Emotional Selectivity. This theory enables us to better understand Karen's concerns. Carstensen considers the relationship among time, motivations, and emotions. She says that as we age, many of us find it difficult maintain all of our previous activities. As time moves on, we may not feel motivated to maintain all of the relationships in our lives. With age we realize that time is limited and that it is important for us to focus energies on activities and relationships that we find enjoyable and satisfying. The key in this process, according to Carstensen, is to understand that there is no right or wrong way to live or age. What is important, she says, is a person's self-awareness. Such self-knowledge enables us to recognize our anxieties. We can then use that recognition to prompt ourselves to engage in those activities that bring us meaning and pleasure (Carstensen, 1993).

If, like Karen, we are unable to recognize that we are overextended, or we no longer find formerly pleasurable activities rewarding, stress begins to overwhelm us. Recognizing our limitations and making changes is one important way of managing stress in our lives. The differences between Simine and Karen illustrate that age is not the only or even the major factor that shapes our perceptions of stress. Even so, there is link that connects chronological age and our perceived time left in life. When we realize that time is limited we also realize that it is important to make the most of that time (Carstensen & Fredrickson, 1998).

Karen slowly begins to recognize that if she wants to be happy, she can no longer do all that she did in the past. She cannot keep pace with her friend Simine who has shown no sign of limiting her social schedule. Karen decides to make some changes. While still staying socially and physically active, she reduces her commitments and curtails her gardening and cooking activities. She and her husband begin to talk about moving to a smaller house. Meanwhile, she begins to take yoga and meditation classes, which help her focus and relax. She is very happy to attend Simine's large parties, but she no longer tries to hold large dinner parties herself.

After making some changes in her life, even small changes, Karen begins to feel less anxious and overwhelmed. Karen and Simine are examples of two women in very similar life circumstances, but who possess different personalities. What makes Simine thrive creates stress for Karen. Because there is no correct way to perceive stress or to recognize what it is doing to us, we must try to tune into our motivations, energies, wishes, and desires.

HOW CAN I BEST MANAGE A MAJOR LIFE CHANGE?

We know that all life experiences can be stressful, but major life events, even positive ones, can lead to anxiety, frustration, and feelings of helplessness. If we are exposed to prolonged stress, we can not only lose our ability to be happy but also our capacity to make adaptive life choices. When a stressor appears, people experience both physical and emotional responses as they attempt to cope with it, which means that it is important to find ways to manage stress so that it is not physically and emotionally overwhelming.

The research of Hans Selye first shed light on the negative impact of stress. Selye studied how the human body reacted to environmental stimuli. More than 60 years ago, Selye (1950) developed the notion of the "fight or flight" response to stress, which was part of what he called "general adaptive syndrome" or GAS, which, in turn, detailed three stages of stress:

1. **The Alarm Stage** — This is made up of a fight-or flight response to a stressful situation. In the alarm state, we recognize a stressor. As our body prepares to deal with it, hormones are released that prime the body to cope with the challenge.

2. **The Resistance Stage** — If the stressor continues, the second stage begins. Selye called this state the resistance stage. In this stage, our bodies operate at a higher rate than normal. They expend energy and effort to cope with the stressor.

3. **The Exhaustion Stage** — If the stressor still persists, the third and final adaptive stage occurs. Selye called this adaptation the exhaustion stage in which we are weary and exhausted. In a state of physical and emotional weariness, we become susceptible to physical and psychological illness.

The stages above provide one way that we can understand the devastating effects of prolonged stress on our lives. Stress is unavoidable, but adequate coping strategies can help us avoid physical and psychological exhaustion.

Here are some examples of what we experience when we are faced with stress.

Physically: Our heart might race; our hands become clammy; we may shake; our breathing becomes rapid and shallow; we may clench our jaw; we might feel light-headed.

Behaviorally: We might find it difficult to concentrate on our work; we experience irritability; we may become angry and fight with our family or friends; we might have trouble sleeping or sleep too much; we might find it difficult to take care of our day-to-day activities — shopping, paying bills, and preparing a meal.

Cognitively: We may not be able to think clearly; our thoughts might race wildly; we may have memory problems; we may ruminate about the cause of the stress that keeps us in a heightened physical state.

Emotionally: We may feel very anxious or fearful; we may feel depressed; we may feel insecure or develop low self-esteem.

WHAT CAN I DO TO MANAGE STRESS?

If we can manage stress effectively, it can help us avoid the debilitating exhaustion Selye (1936) discussed. In this process, the first step is to identify what seems stressful to you. As stated earlier, what is stressful to one person is not necessary stressful for others. What we find stressful is based on our "appraisal" of the situation. A well-known theory of understanding stress, discussed later in this chapter, addresses the importance of appraisal in how stress affects us. Stress is highly subjective. The case of Suzanna and April illustrates varying ways of viewing some of the stressors experienced in later life.

Suzanna and April, both in their 60s, voluntarily chose to retire. No one pressured them to do so. After teaching for 30 years, they both decided that they wanted a change. Even though retirement is a major life-changing transition, Suzanna is happy about the coming changes in her life. She has many hobbies that keep her busy. She has a large circle of friends and family with whom she spends time. She also works out regularly. In short, she has planned for her retirement and is pleased with her decision.

With every life change there is an adjustment period. Suzanna anticipated this period. When she experiences discomfort or anxiety, she acknowledges it and goes for a walk or keeps herself busy in other ways. In this way, her anxiety soon dissipates. After just a few weeks of her retirement, she developed a flexible schedule for herself. She signed up for exercise classes three times a week. Four days a week, she arranged a walk with friends in the neighborhood. She planned an extended vacation and joined a reading group. After three months of the retired life, she wondered how she ever found time to work 40 hours a week. She was active, busy and happy with the new stage of her life.

April also looked forward to retirement. Once she retired and spent a couple of weeks resting, she became increasingly anxious. She could not seem to bring herself to engage in all the activities she had looked forward to prior to retirement. As each day passed she wondered how she could escape her sense of lethargy. She felt unmotivated and unsatisfied with her retirement experience. She even began to regret her decision to retire. After talking with her husband and friends, she realized that she was not ready for full-time retirement. She went back to substitute teaching two days a week. When she started to work part-time, she felt much better. Part-time teaching increases the pleasure she derives from the freedom she has on the other days of the week. She quickly understood that she was not ready for full-time retirement and was able to make the changes that would meet her needs.

Personality differences shaped how these women adjusted to retirement. Suzanna had always been extroverted and found it easy to make new friends and start new projects. April, by contrast had always preferred more structure. She always found it difficult to deal with major changes in her life. Until she retired, she had not been aware of this personal fact. She had to admit to herself that it was difficult for her to create her own schedule. Instead of seeing the process as a positive challenge like Suzanna, April saw it as unsatisfying and stressful.

Once April realized how she was responding to this major life transition, she learned new ways of coping with her stressful response and made changes that resulted in a happy part-time retirement. Many of us are not aware of what we find stressful and how we might respond to a new situation until we find ourselves unable to manage a stressful life event.

Self-assessment is an important way of understanding what we might find stressful. Consider the following:

1. Make a list of major life events that you have experienced in the past three years.
2. How do you feel about these events?
3. Are they manageable?
4. Do you have resources to cope with them?
5. Have these events been planned or are they unexpected?
6. How did you react to them?
7. Do you ruminate about the event?
8. Did you feel helpless about managing the event?

Once you have asked yourself some of these questions and made a list of the stressors in your life, think about how you might improve your coping skills.

Remember stress is a normal part of life. Without stress our lives would be uninteresting. Stress can motivate us to make positive changes. Experiencing a certain amount of stress tends to be protective and adaptive. If it is not overwhelming, stress can lead us to optimum performance. Too little stress can lead to stagnation, a lack of motivation, or a decreased interest in life. Stress can be positive or negative. Distress is the state of continuously feeling anxious, helpless, and overwhelmed. Eustress, by contrast, is positive and can motivate and challenge us.

TOO MUCH OR TOO LITTLE STRESS IS HARMFUL TO OUR HEALTH AND HAPPINESS

Stress is unavoidable in life. As Hans Selye (1936) and many other stress researchers over the decades have demonstrated, too much stress leads to exhaustion, illness, unhappiness, and even death. The amount of stress a person can tolerate varies with individual personality and the personal and social resources available. These include the presence of social support and healthful environmental conditions. For some individuals, stress can lead to growth and change. For other people, it can lead to illness and even death.

STRESS AND COPING

1. The effects of stress are dependent upon the interaction between who you are and the environment in which you live.
2. The ways in which stress affects you does not depend on the stress itself but on how you evaluate it.

Lazarus and Folkman (1984) studied how people cope with stress. They introduced the "appraisal theory" of stress. This theory states that our perception of a particular event as stressful is central to how we react to it. For example: If our car breaks down and requires $1,000 of inconvenient repairs, we may or may not be stressed. If we have been prepared to purchase a new car or planned for the expense in our budget but didn't want to trade in a perfectly well-functioning car, then the breakdown may be just what we wanted. The breakdown motivates us to finally treat ourselves to that new car. On the other hand, if, like most people, we need our car, cannot afford a new one, and find the repair bill to be rather steep; the breakdown would be perceived as a very stressful event. The key element here is not the car breaking down but our reaction to this event and our ability (time and money) to deal with the breakdown.

The diagram below illustrates the importance of what Folkman and Lazarus refer to as "appraisal."

A	B	C
Stressful Event	Belief about the Event	Consequences

The belief you have about a stressful event has more impact on the consequences of stress on your health and well-being than the actual stressful event.

THE WAYS IN WHICH WE MANAGE STRESS CAN BE DIVIDED INTO 3 CATEGORIES:

1. Appraisal-focused coping — redefining the meaning of the stressor
2. Problem-focused coping — change or eliminate stress
3. Emotional focus — managing the emotion aroused by stress

Everyone engages in all three ways of coping with stress. Whether or not we are doing what is best for us depends on the particular stressor. Studies have shown that there are age-related differences in the strategies for dealing with stress. For example:
1. Younger adults tend to use more problem-oriented approaches, where they attempt to directly change the stressful situation.

2. Older adults, on the other hand, tend to worry less about problems they cannot change. They also tend to use more emotion-focused problem solving. This means that they try to change the way they look at or approach a problem.
3. Older people generally become more mature in the ways they cope with stress.
4. Older adults also report having fewer stressors in their lives.

WHAT ARE SOME MATURE/POSITIVE WAYS OF DEALING WITH STRESS?

1. Use humor
2. Spend time outside, commune with nature
3. Cultivate positive emotions
4. Increase your flexibility
5. Maintain hope and optimism
6. Cultivate social relationships and support
7. The talking cure — talk it out
8. Live in the present, remember the past, and make plans for the future
9. Stress and Health

Studies indicate almost 50% of Americans have experienced stress-related health problems. Many of our visits to physicians can be linked to stress. Stress is also linked to heart disease, cancer, and suicide. Stress also results in unhappiness and premature aging. Each year stress exacts an expensive financial and emotional toll on Americans. Granted, it is not possible to eliminate stressors from one's life, but stress adaptation techniques, such as time management, relaxation, meditation, and mindfulness, can help prevent these stressors from becoming destructive. The remaining chapters of this book will discuss some of the important stressors of later life and present some ways that we might manage those stressors so that our happiness and well-being is not derailed.

REFERENCES

+   Carstensen, L. L. (1993). *Motivation for social contact across the life span: A theory of socio-emotional selectivity.* (pp. 209-254) University of Nebraska Press, Lincoln, NE.

+   Carstensen, L. L., & Fredrickson, B. L. (1998). Influence of HIV status and age on cognitive representations of others. *Health Psychology, 17(6),* 494-503.

+   Holmes, T. H., & Rahe, R. H. (1967). The Social Readjustment Rating Scale. *Journal of Psychosomatic Research, 11(2),* 213-218.

+   Lazarus, R.S., & Folkman, S. (1984). *Stress, appraisal, and coping.* New York: Springer.

+   Selye, H. (1936). "A syndrome produced by diverse nocuous agents." *Nature,* 138, 32.

+   Selye, H., & Fortier, C. (1950). Adaptive reactions to stress. *Research Publications of the Association for Research in Nervous & Mental Disease, 29,* 3-18.

CHAPTER TWO

The Time of Our Life

CHAPTER TWO

The Time of Our Life

Like most Americans, I frequently find myself rushing from place to place. There is too much to do and not enough time to do it. Modern life is busier and more hectic than previous times. The lack of time makes people feel anxious and tense. When there is no relief from the fast pace of one's obligations, our health begins to suffer. As a psychologist who studies health and aging, I have often wondered if there is a way for us to successfully step off the merry-go-round, or at least take restorative breaks. There are, of course, "off the grid" movements, or movements in which people choose to live without modern conveniences, which, in turn, put them beyond the reach of technology. While this choice sounds appealing for a short period of time, it is not something that most people desire in the long run. Even if we did desire it, it would be difficult to follow the "off the grid" path. Most of us do not want to be isolated from meaningful work, a supportive family, or from a reaffirming circle of friends.

Is it possible to live a more relaxed life without moving off the grid? In this chapter, I discuss the relationship between modernization and technology, and work time and free time. I will suggest small steps that we can take to better manage our time. I am, of course, no exception to the pressures of modern life. Anxiety continuously seeps its way into my life. I often feel the need to rush from place to place. I live in a congested area, and crowds make me uncomfortable, which means that I alter my schedule to avoid crowds. I get up earlier to walk. I eat later to avoid the dinner rush. I schedule my teaching during rush hour to avoid a busy commute. I am grateful to have a flexible work schedule. Planning is one way to manage stress in life. Planning usually works well for me, but when it does not, which of course also happens, I experience anxiety and stress.

To prepare for this chapter, I interviewed several older men and women, some retired and some who still work full or part time. I had anticipated that the retired men and women would be more relaxed. I assumed that retirees would not experience the same time pressure as those who had work commitments.

Surprisingly, I found no difference. It seems that retirement does little to slow the hectic pace of modern life. I will discuss stress and retirement more fully in the next chapter, but it seems that retirement status does not significantly influence one's relationship with time.

Sharon retired two years ago. As a busy and successful lawyer, she worked 50 plus hours a week, which meant that she had little time for relaxation. In precious moments of spare time, she went the gym, trying to stay in shape. Pressed for time, dinners often consisted of a frozen meal. Time constrained her vacations to two 5-day weekends a year: one at the beach and one visiting her grandparents in Colorado. On both of these "vacation" trips she took her computer and felt compelled to spend several hours a day "at work." This hectic professional pace took its toll in the form of a divorce. Time obligations meant that she and her first husband rarely saw one another. They grew apart.

Sharon recently got remarried and wants to spend more time with her new husband, Steve, an architect, who was laid off from his job and now works part-time as a consultant. Happy with his scaled-down schedule, Steve wanted Sharon to spend more time with him. Anticipating that she would be have all the time in the world to do what she wanted, Sharon decided to take early retirement. Retirement confounded her expectations; she is still rushing from place to place. She still feels anxious about time-constrained days. Although she makes plans to travel, see friends, and exercise, her schedule occasionally make her irritable.

Eventually Sharon and Steve concluded they needed help. They want to have an active and happy life, but somehow a lifetime of rushing about prevented them from being able to relax and enjoy their retirement. They employed a life coach who works with them to develop a more flexible schedule that balances responsibility and pleasure. The coach helped Sharon view time differently. She suggested they make a ranked list of activities they find necessary and activities they enjoy. The life coach encouraged them to free themselves of the items at the bottom of their lists. After several weeks, Sharon and Steve felt more comfortable. They are still busy. Sharon, in fact, decided she was not fully ready for retirement. She took a part-time job. Sharon and Steve are learning to think differently about time and responsibilities. If a day goes by and they do not get anything done, it is OK. If a friend stops by for an unplanned visit, they learn to enjoy the unexpected. When they feel stressed because they are running behind schedule, they remind each other that it is OK. Slowly they began to feel more relaxed — and happier. They even "schedule" one free day a week. They make their way through this day with no plans. They do what they choose to do, either together or alone.

STRESS AND TIME

The results of contemporary social research indicate that lack of time is one of key stress triggers for many Americans. In one of my early jobs as a clinical psychologist working at a University Counseling Center, I was responsible for developing stress management programs. "Lessons in time management" was one of the most popular workshops. In these workshops, we hoped to teach young adults

how to effectively manage their time. The results of numerous studies suggested that our efforts were not successful. A perceived lack of time — especially free time — is pervasive. Time pressure leads to a number of negative consequences — physical aches and pains, strains on social relationships, a decrease in the quality of one's work.

Lack of time also manifests itself in an individual's inability to take a vacation or to do rejuvenating nothing for a period of time. This is surprising given that evidence indicates if people work more productively, they are healthier, happier, and less stressed. It is evident that taking time off increases productivity and promotes well-being and happiness.

In our wired world, most people spend their time multitasking — rushing from place to place, answering emails and texts. There are very few moments in life in which we are not bombarded with technological demands. The itch to respond to these demands has accelerated the already fast pace of life. These days free time is a rare commodity. It is a rare moment indeed when we can do exactly what we want or spend time in a purposeful lack of activity. Increasingly, Americans are engaged in long hours of arduous work (Gini, 2003).

VACATIONS ARE IMPORTANT

As summer draws to a close, many people frantically struggle to find the time for a last-minute holiday break. These frantic plans often lead to one long weekend at the beach. Industrialization was supposed to increase our free time. While industrialization has improved the quality of life in many ways —advanced medical care, systematic sanitation, and improved systems of communication — it has also created greater time constraints (Garhammer, 2002). Although the United States is the most industrialized country in the word, Americans have fewer vacation days than any other technologically advanced country. Studies show that many Americans are even afraid to take the vacation days they have earned for fear of falling behind in their work or being perceived as un-motivated (Weber, 2004).

Social scientists know that vacations are an important ingredient in the recipe for a happy and fulfilled life. They increase life satisfaction and promote physical and psychological health. When we skip vacations, the lack of unencumbered free time leads to an increased risk for depression and heart disease. Unfortunately, when Americans do manage to get away, it is usually a long weekend during which they remained "connected" through computers, iPhones, and iPads. Vacations have become as frantic as workdays. People cram a wide variety of "leisure" activities — days at the beach, holiday visits, going to amusement parks, or taking hiking trips — into one long four-day weekend. They return to work exhausted, which compounds the overwhelming demands of work and home.

WHAT IS FREE TIME?

Free time is time devoted to leisure or recreation. Leisure is derived from the Latin word licere, meaning "to be permitted" or "to be free." Free time activities can be active or passive, social or solitary. Free time can help alleviate stress. It leads to rejuvenation, renewal, improved life satisfaction and increased happiness (Ponde & Santana, 2000). Americans spend an average of 1,800 hours a year at the office, the factory, the store, or the farm. This amount is more than the rest of the industrialized world. Germans work an average 1,350 per year — almost 500 fewer hours than the American worker.

FREE TIME AND INDUSTRIALIZATION

Our current understanding of "free time" is connected to the Industrial Revolution. Modernization and industrialization changed the way people had lived for centuries. In pre-industrial times, light and the seasons loosely structured a person's time. Industrialization resulted in more structured days. People adhered to a working schedule, spending their working hours at a factory or office. Non-working hours, time spent with family and friends were supposedly devoted to

leisure and recreation. Because machines were doing more of the work, the notion was that people would have more free time.

Over the course of time, it appears that an inverse pattern emerged. In the industrial and post-industrial ages, a person's free time has been steadily declining (Glover & Hemingway, 2005). Increased industrialization and technological advancements have led to a decrease in free time. In the wake of these social developments, there has been a steep increase in stress-related physical and psychological health disorders. We are working longer hours, taking fewer days off and becoming "sicker" as a consequence.

Michael is 56-year-old electrical engineer. He has worked for the same company for 18 years. His work requires him to travel several days a month during which he spends nights in sterile chain hotels. During his work travel, he misses the comforts of home and family. When he is home, he tries to spend as much time as possible with his family. He has two grown children and one grandchild. Michael always dreamed that one day he and his wife would be able to buy or at least rent a cabin on a lake where his children and grandchildren could spend their holidays. He has enough money to invest in a small vacation home but does not have the time to find a place. Sometimes, he feels that his colleagues see him as "old" and out of date. He is afraid that if he takes even two of his allotted four weeks' vacation they might think he is expendable. So even if he did have his little cottage on a lake, would he have the time to actually enjoy it? Would his children and grandchild have the time and desire to visit? When they visited would everyone be on their computers and iPhones instead of spending family time? Michael is worried that if he does not take steps toward realizing his dream, it will soon be too late. He or his wife could become chronically ill. They could become too ill to swim or canoe on a lake — two of his fantasies.

Michael's situation is not unusual. On average, American vacations have decreased to less than five days (Elliot, 2003). Perhaps this decrease in free time explains why one in every three Americans states that they "always" feel rushed (Elliot, 2003). In the industrialized world, the United States averages the fewest number of vacation days — an average of nine days. In Japan, which has the next lowest rate of vacation, workers get eighteen days off each year.

Free time is made up of:
1. A chosen activity
2. Non-obligatory activity
3. Recreation
4. Play
5. Restful rejuvenation
6. Enjoyable

There is no one way to spend one's free time. There are different ways. Free time activities are based on personality, age, gender, individual history, culture, personal interests. Categories include:
1. Cultural activities: concerts, sporting events, community involvement
2. Physical activities: golf, hiking, walking, and gardening
3. Social activities: visiting with friends, family
4. Solitary activities: reading and watching TV

INEQUALITY AND FREE TIME

There is a free time famine in the United States. This famine affects some segments of the population more severely than others. For example, men and women from lower socio-economic status experience greater financial constraints that constrain their participation in free time activities (Henderson & Alnsworth, 2003). Working men have more time off than working women. Those with more control over their work are better able to take time off. A lack of control over one's time can lead to anxiety and depression. Although there are exceptions, some people thrive on a fast-paced, stressful day-to-day routine. In general, the faster the pace of one's life the more stress related conditions one tends to experience. In an interesting book that explores time, Levine (1997) concluded that the faster the pace of life in a city, the higher the rates of coronary heart disease. Levine also discusses the relationship between a slower pace of life and happiness.

Is a slower pace of life the panacea for modern stress? The answer, according to Levine's book, is not clear-cut. In many cases, people in a slower paced city or culture are happier. However there appears to be a "pace of life" paradox. Although a fast pace of life can lead to stress-related concerns, a faster pace of life can also lead to greater productivity that can marginally improve a person's life. Even so, when the pace of life is overwhelming, the quality of life is diminished.

TIME IS MONEY

Americans seem to view time as a commodity that should not be wasted. One in every five US workers currently feels as if their work is either "very stressful" or "extremely stressful," and close to 70% of Americans say that they would like to have more free time. In fact, 63% of people go so far as to say that they would rather have more time off than money (Lopez, 2000). Despite these desires, the recession and the on-going threat of layoffs have led to cultural expectations that make people fearful of taking time off from work — no matter how much time off they've earned or how much they need to relax and recuperate.

Accordingly, many Americans feel that they desperately need more time off but are afraid to take it. In fact, even if they are sick, many people feel they have to go to work. In this time-pressured atmosphere, many Americans who have earned time off do not use all of their vacation days (Donnan, 2005). A 2003 study of 730 US executives revealed that 58% cited job pressures as the reason for not taking allotted time off (Weber, 2004). Social norms and public and private policies reinforce this relentless work ethic.

MANDATING VACATION DAYS

The United States is the only industrialized country that does not mandate vacation days for its workers (Francis, 2006). In comparison, France not only mandates a 35-hour workweek, but also allots over four weeks for vacations each year. Germany, Spain, Australia, Italy, and other developed nations all mandate at least twenty vacation days a year for their workers (Francis, 2006). Japan, with the

lowest number of days off after the United States, allows its workers an average of 18 days of vacation per year. In the US, by contrast, employers are generally not required to provide vacation days for their employees. Japan and the United States share a relatively fast pace of life, but interestingly enough, Japan has a low rate of coronary heart disease, which sets it apart from the United States (Brislin & Kim, 2003). Perhaps more time away from work is one of the reasons for this difference?

In Europe, holidays tend to be viewed as a social right. In the month of August, as many as 50% of Europeans are on vacation. In the US, vacations are seen as an inconvenience and even a problem for employers.

Mark works for a large company as a director of marketing. His busiest time is July and August. In more than 20 years of working for the same company, Mark has never taken a week off during these precious summer months when his children are out of school. Mark is bitter and regretful about this but feels unable to change his situation. He's planning an earlier retirement than he would like. He wants to enjoy his summers.

Like Mark, many Americans who do have vacations tend to see them as a privilege not a right. They have to "earn" their time off. As workers spend more time with the same employer, their small-allocation time off tends to increase minimally. On average, after one year of employment, a person may be given approximately nine paid days off. After twenty years of continued service, these days increase to an average of nineteen. In the US, a high value is placed on work and wealth often at the expense of health and well-being. Clearly, attitudes about free time in the US should be re-evaluated.

HISTORICAL BACKGROUND OF WORKING HOURS IN THE UNITED STATES

In the United States, attitudes about work derive from the Protestant work ethic. Americans have a long history of working many hours a week. In the 1800s, in a mostly agricultural country, many Americans seasonally worked their fields for over seventy hours per week. During the non-agricultural parts of the year, however, people lived at slower pace. They had time for rest and renewal. With the spread of industrialization in the late 19th century, employers began to order their employees, usually immigrants, women, and even children, to work long hours, six days a week. In the early 1900s, even children under the age of 6 were working in Pennsylvania coal mines.

Even by today's standards, the aforementioned typical workweek was long and brutal. In 1904, the National Child Labor Committee, which was dedicated to the abolition of child labor, was formed in the United States. The "Progressive Era" in the US (1900-1920s) was a period of rapid growth, mass immigration and an increased awareness of the poor working conditions in America — especially for immigrants, women, and children (Mutari, Power, & Figart, 2002).

During this time minimum wage laws, which initially excluded women, were passed. Working conditions improved somewhat. In 1924, the US Congress attempted to pass a law that would prohibit child labor, although it was not until 1938, when President Franklin D. Roosevelt signed the Fair Labor Standards Act, that limits were finally placed on child labor.

The length of the workweek became dramatically shorter during the years spanning WWI, resulting in a six-day workweek of eight-hour days. In 1926, the 5-day workweek was implemented. Even as the workweek officially shortened and quality of life improved, the expected expansion of free time did not fully materialize in the United States.

Contemporary American social norms still associate positive qualities with those who work persistently. For fear of not being taken seriously, people are afraid to discuss their vacations at work. Contemporary Americans find themselves stressed by the very things they regard highly (Peterson, 2004). In short, the work ethic is still central to the dominant value system of the United States (Glover & Hemingway, 2005). One study indicated that 67% of children want their parents to work fewer hours (Negrey, 2004). The majority of adults in the US wished they had more time off, more flexible working hours, and paid annual leave and vacation time. Considering these wishes, it is unfortunate that there is such a poverty of free time in the United States.

RETIREMENT AND FREE TIME

Age and gender shape perceptions of free time. The economic downturn of the first decade of the 21st century has resulted in an increasing number of Americans who postpone retirement. By choice or necessity, Americans continue to work. These older workers experience more anxiety about taking time off than their younger counterparts. They fear reprisals from ageist stereotypes, which means they struggle to work long hours. They don't want their younger colleagues to think they are ill or too "tired" to work. As a result, they avoid taking time off from work. Older adults also carry the work habits of an earlier generation. Studies

show that older workers are more reliable, punctual, take fewer sick days and have a higher work commitment than younger workers. By 2014, 41% of Americans 55 or older will be still be working. These older workers will make up over 21% of the US labor force.

Older workers, regardless of the degree of the commitment, also need free time to re-charge their batteries. Age-related changes can raise adaptive challenges for older working adults. Many older workers who do not take time off can become overwhelmed and find themselves at increased risk for illness, injury, disability, and diminished productivity. With increasing age, free time becomes even more important to health and happiness.

THE GENDERED NATURE OF FREE TIME

Women tend to have fewer opportunities for free time than men who work (Mattingly & Bianchi, 2003). In 1995, 46% of the American workforce consisted of women. By 2007, this figure had reached 61.4% (Negrey, 2004). The largest increase in the labor force was related to an increase in working mothers (Hayghe, 1997). Nearly one in every five employed parents is single. The same percentage falls into the category of the "Sandwich Generation," which consists of middle-aged adults, generally women, who are caring for an older family member.

Women not only work full time but they still do most of the work in a household, including the lion's share of childcare. Women's free time is a function of their multiple social roles (Shannon & Shaw, 2005). Care-giving responsibilities for elderly parents and grandchildren are responsibilities that tend to fall to older female adults. Most mothers say that they spend almost all of their free time with their children. Fathers, by contrast devote only 28% of their free time with their offspring. Even when women do manage to have the time to take a vacation, they are usually burdened with the preparation of meals, housework, childcare, and elder care.

Working women are also frequently employed in lower status positions. Such positions require longer working hours with fewer days off ("The conundrum of the glass ceiling," 2005). When employers make a reduction of working hours available, women tend to avail themselves of the opportunity, often not to participate in free time activities, but to fulfill the aforementioned responsibilities.

Many women do not remember when they last had a free day. A Real Simple study surveyed how American women spend their free time (free time was defined as time spent on yourself, where you can choose to do the things you enjoy). The results showed that more than half of American women say they do not have enough free time. Fifty-two percent say they have less than 90 minutes of free time a day; 28% say they have less than 45 minutes a day. When they do have free time they are often interrupted by family or work demands ("How do women spend their time?" 2011).

MANAGING TIME

1. Make a list of how you spend your days
2. Remove one thing from your list
3. Spend the time you saved on yourself, on an activity you enjoy or lack of activity
4. After a week, remove one more item from your list
5. Make certain that you eat at least one of your meals sitting down while focusing on enjoying your food
6. Indulge yourself
7. Learn to let go
8. Everything does not have to be done well

WORK PATTERNS ACROSS THE LIFESPAN

Work patterns are best understood from a life course perspective. As roles and responsibilities change, working hours vary across the adult lifespan. Younger adults, who are struggling to begin their careers, tend to work significantly more than the typical forty-hour workweek (Costa & Di Milia, 2008). Midlife is a time when a worker tends to be most productive and successful. Erikson (1994) calls midlife a period referred of generativity. It is a time when adults are concerned with making a contribution to society. This contribution can take a variety of forms, including creative endeavors, professional commitment, contributions to one's community, and/or rearing children (Erikson, 1994). It is also a time during which caring for others is at its peak. The generational squeeze experienced by midlife women has been well documented. These dual commitments often leave midlife women physically and psychologically exhausted.

Many modern Americans view later adulthood, or the retirement period, as the only time when they can slow down and rest. "The golden years" may be the only long awaited and a hard-earned time of rest and relaxation (Tahmaseb-McConatha, et al., 2003). As mentioned in Chapter 1, after a lifetime of hard work, it may be difficult to finally profit from the free time of later adulthood. Rest and relaxation may be so unfamiliar that older women and men may find it difficult to enjoy it all. Staying active and physically engaged is important to health and happiness during retirement. Active engagement with one's world is not contradictory to also having time to slow down, be mindful, and relax. A lack of experience and awareness about how to relax may prevent retired men and women from enjoying these years fully. Just as work habits need to be learned, slowing down and being more mindful also takes practice, but the rewards are immeasurable.

Regardless of the time of life, it appears that Americans have been unable to utilize free time to cope with the stress in their lives. To be happier and healthier, as well as more productive, they must change their attitudes about free time and vacations. Perhaps we should look at free time as a basic human right rather than a luxury.

AN IDEAL VACATION?

People choose their vacations based on their:
1. Economic circumstances
2. Health
3. Personal expectations
4. Where they live
5. Personality
6. Culture

Free time or leisure interests are developed early in life. A large part of childhood is taken up with leisure or play. Interests change, but we should tune into our likes, preferences, and wishes.

1. Learn what makes you happy through self-awareness (includes awareness of your personality)
2. Your subjective evaluation designates an activity as leisure (one person's leisure vs. another's leisure).
3. Free time is a way to renew the self; it is also a way to recreate the self.
4. Make plans and decisions based on your true self.
5. Tune into feelings/thoughts.
6. Avoid the "tyranny of the should."

Free time or leisure activities are successful if they produce a feeling of "flow" (Csikszenthihalyi, 1990). When a person becomes completely immersed in an activity, they have experienced flow. In a flow experience, one temporarily loses her or his sense of self and becomes totally involved in an activity. Csikszentmihalyi (1990) suggests that people are happiest when they are engaged in a sense of flow in which their whole being is involved, which in turn results in feeling energized and motivated.

Flow is different for each person. One can experience flow by walking, running, reading, skiing, talking with friends, listening to music, or playing music. These are activities in which you employ a set of skills that provide you with a sense of

absorption and challenge. While only a small percentage of people experience flow on a regular basis, engaging in more free time can increase the possibility of experiencing it.

CHARACTERISTICS OF FLOW

1. Total concentration and enjoyment
2. Lack of self-consciousness
3. Being fully engaged in an activity
4. Being engaged in a balanced challenge and skill (too much challenge may produce anxiety, too little challenge may lead to boredom)

American norms and values are filled with messages of the importance of dedication to hard work. There is an adage: idle hands are the devil's workshop. This deeply ingrained value gave shape and texture to the issues articulated in this chapter. The notion of "idle hands" makes many working men and women think twice about taking a vacation. In much of the rest of the world, there is a greater emphasis and even prestige associated with leisure and downtime.

Clearly free time, down time, time for relaxation, and time for vacations are important for everyone's health and well-being. During the recent recession it became popular to say that one was taking a "staycation." This indicated time off for relaxation at home, avoiding the expense of travel. However, studies indicate that very few Americans actually took their time off either at a holiday location or at home, much to the detriment of their health and happiness. This chapter has addressed the importance of free time for positive physical and emotional development — regardless of the stage of life. Even so, as the body ages it needs more opportunity for rest and renewal. Take a vacation; it will make you healthier and happier. It does not matter what you do. Spend a couple of days in pajamas.

FREE TIME HAS NUMEROUS BENEFITS

1. It maintains or renews ties with others
2. It alleviates or prevents depression (through flow, concentration, challenge)
3. It contributes to overall well-being and happiness
4. It renews and energizes us

IF YOU DO NOT KNOW WHAT TO DO WITH YOUR FREE TIME, ANALYZE WHAT YOU ENJOY

1. Pay attention to how you spend your days; write down the major activities you engage in.
2. Make a list of necessary activities, measure the amount of time you spend on each.
3. Then make a list of the activities you enjoy
4. Evaluate how often you do these enjoyable things
   frequently = 3; occasionally = 2; sometimes = 1
   If your sum of these scores is 12 to 15, you are doing OK; higher than 15, you are in good shape; but below 12, you should seriously evaluate how you spend your days.
5. Increase what you like, decrease what you dislike and do not have to do. Deliberately add enjoyable free time or leisure to your life.

REASONS TO ENJOY FREE TIME

1. Remember your roots/past/interests
2. Follow what your feelings, thoughts, listen to what your intuitions tell you
3. Develop flexible goals and plans that include time off
4. Live in the present
5. It's OK to change, stay tuned to changes in your interests
6. Acknowledge your dreams before it is too late

REFERENCES

+ Brislin R.W., & Kim, E.S. (2003). Cultural Diversity in People's Understanding and Uses of Time. *Applied Psychology: An International Review*, 52 (3), 363-382.

+ Csíkszentmihályi, Mihály (1990), *Flow: The Psychology of Optimal Experience*, New York: Harper and Row.

+ Costa, G. & Di Milia, L. (2008). Aging and Shift work: a complex problem to face. *Chronobiology International*, 25(2&3), 165-181.

+ Donnan, C. (2005). Mental Health at Work. *Occupational Health*, 57, 2-5.

+ Elliot, C. (2003). Vanishing vacations: shorter and more costly. *USA Today*, July 23, 13a.

+ Erikson, E.H. (1994). *Identity and the Life Cycle*. W.W. Norton & Company: New York.

+ Francis, D. (2006). Why the U.S. should mandate paid vacations. *Christian Science Monitor*, 98, 176.

+ Garhammer, M. (2002). Pace of life and enjoyment of life. *Journal of Happiness Studies*, 3, 212-256.

+ Gini, A. (2003). *The Importance of Being Lazy*. (93) Routledge: New York.

+ Glover, T., & Hemingway, J. (2005). Locating leisure in the social capital literature. *Journal of Leisure Research, 37* (4), 387-401.

+ Hayghe, H.V. (1997). Developments in Women's Labor Force Participation. *Monthly Labor Review*, 120 (9), 41-46.

+ Henderson, K., & Alnsworth, B. (2003). A synthesis of perceptions about physical activity among older African-American and American-Indian women. *American Journal of Public Health, 93* (2), 313-318.

+ How do women spend their time? 2001. Retrieved October 10, 2013 from http://www.realsimple.com/work-life/life-strategies/time-management/spend-time-00100000077167/

+ Jorgensen, H. (2002). Give Me A Break: The Extent of Paid Holidays and Vacation. *Center for Economic and Policy Research, 2-10*.

+ Levine, R. (1997). *A Geography of Time*. New York: Basic.

+ Levine, R. (1999). The Pace of Life in 31 Countries. *Journal of Cross Cultural Psychology*, 30, 178-205.

+ Lopez, S. (2000). What you need is more vacation. *Time, 155*, 24.

+ Mattingly, M., & Sayer, L.(2006) Under pressure: gender differences in the relationship between free time and feeling rushed. *Journal of Marriage and Family, 68* (1).

+ Mattingly, M., & Bianchi, S. (2003). Gender differences in the quantity and quality of free time: the U.S. experience. *Social Forces, 81* (3), 999-1030.

+ Mutari, E., Power, M., & Figart, D. (2002). Neither mothers nor breadwinners: African-American women's exclusion from U.S. minimum wage policies, 1912-38. *Feminist Economics, 8* (2), 37-61.

+ Negrey, C. (2004). A new full-time norm: promoting work-life integration through work-time adjustment. *Institute for Women's Policy Research* (IWPR Publication No. C357). Washington, DC.

+ Peterson, M., & Wilson, J. (2004). Work stress in America. *International Journal of Stress Management, 11* (2), 91-113.

+ Ponde, M., & Santana, V. (2000). Participation in leisure activities: is it a protective factor for women's mental health. *Journal of Leisure Research, 32* (4), 457-473.

+ Shannon, C., & Shaw, S. (2005). "If the dishes don't get done today, they'll get done tomorrow": a breast cancer experience as a catalyst for changes to women's leisure. *Journal of Leisure Research, 37* (2), 195-215.

+ Tahmaseb-McConatha, J., Volkwein, K.. & Schnell, F., Leach, E., Riley, L. (2003) Attitudes Toward Aging: A Comparative Analysis of Young Adults from the united States and Germany. *The International Journal of Aging and Human Development, 57,* (3), 203-215.

+ Tahmaseb-McConatha, J., Volkwein, K., Vita, M.E., Mauriello, M., & DiGregorio, N. (2009). American and German men and women discuss retirement: A qualitative study. *Open Journal of Psychology, 2,* 1-7.

+ The conundrum of the glass ceiling. (2005). *The Economist, 376* (8436). Weber, G. (2004). Lost time: vacation days go unused despite more liberal time-off policies. *Workforce Management, 83,* 13.

CHAPTER THREE

Coping with Retirement

CHAPTER THREE

Coping with Retirement

Retirement is one of the most important transitions in social life. Similar to getting married, graduating, having children, or beginning a career, retirement influences every aspect of one's life. Achieving a happy and satisfying retirement is therefore very important for the establishment and reinforcement of well-being and happiness in later life. Even so, a positive transition to retirement can be a challenge. There are no specific guidelines for a happy retirement. During the retirement years, each person will experience different joys, satisfactions, and stressors. There are, however, common factors that shape the retirement experience. In this chapter, I address some of these factors and provide practical suggestions on ways to cope with some of the concerns that retired men and women commonly confront.

The Case of Phillip

Phillip is in his late 50s. For the last 20 years, he has worked for the same bank. As the bank's senior vice president, he has had a good income and good benefits. His children are now in college. Once the balance of college bills has been reduced to zero, he and his wife Sandy look forward to travelling. In the prime of his life, Phillip expected to work for another 10 years. Then the unexpected occurred. A larger company bought Phillip's bank. The new management team decided to dismiss Phillip's entire department. Phillip was devastated. He had always been a conscientious worker. Still unemployed, he questions his self-worth. He finds himself depressed and anxious. After several weeks of lying around the house, Phillip realizes he must make some changes. With Sandy's help, he begins to reassess his situation. They gradually come to the conclusion that Phillip might be ready for retirement. If he and Sandy sold their house, they could still afford to purchase a smaller house, pay off their children's tuition, and travel. They took action. Indeed, one year after being laid off, Phillip is back to his confident self. He consults on a part-time basis and enjoys the flexibility that retirement affords. Although his income has decreased, he feels happier and is less stressed.

Personal circumstances and social factors influence how happy one is during the retirement years. Financial worries, health concerns, and care-giving responsibilities are among the top three retirement stressors. The first concern when considering retirement should be an assessment of the reasons for retirement and an analysis of plans for retirement.

Important retirement considerations

- Have you planned for your retirement?
- What are the top three reasons for your retirement?
- Are you retiring by choice?
- Are you looking forward to life after retirement? Do you feel ready?
- Recognize that the reason for retiring will influence your experience. Be aware of this factor and make necessary adjustments.

- Are you retiring to care for an ill parent or family member?
- Do you have health concerns?
- Do you have adequate income?
- Do you have goals and/or plans for your retirement?
- Are your goals and plans based on who you are as a person? For example: If you have never golfed, you probably will not enjoy a golf-filled retirement.
- How have you dealt with your previous life transitions? Be prepared to have similar reactions.
- Remember it will take time to adjust to retirement.
- Be prepared for trial and error in your planning.

RETIREMENT TODAY

The image of an older person sitting on a porch relaxing in a rocking chair is no longer a realistic view of retirement. By the same token, retirement is still seen as a time of life when one is free from work responsibilities and free to engage more fully in leisure and recreational activities. The retirement years should prove to be satisfying and fulfilling. But if one is not ready for retirement, if retirement is unexpected, undesired, and/or unplanned, it can be one of the most stressful times in life.

Contemporary retirement scenarios are very different from those of even a few years ago. Today's retired men and women are usually healthier, wealthier, and happier than their forbearers. Given the influence of various organizations that advocate for the rights of older people, they are more powerful and influential. For example, the American Association of Retired Persons (AARP) is a powerful organization that advocates for the rights of older Americans. Ethel Percy Andrus founded AARP in 1958 as a non-profit organization designed to serve the needs of older adults. Today AARP has more than 40 million members and is a powerful lobbying organization that focuses its attention on health insurance, entertainment, travel, insurance, education, poverty, and other factors that influencing the well-being of older Americans.

Today's retirees are also more physically active than the elders of previous generations. They exercise, hike, walk, run, practice yoga, work out on machines, swim, and travel extensively.

These active retirees are living life to the fullest. Unfortunately, many older adults do not exercise regularly (Tahmaseb-McConatha & Volkwein-Caplan, 2012). Regardless of life circumstances, exercise is one of the best ways to maintain both physical and psychological health. In fact, a recent New York Times article from October 15, 2013, stated that a structured exercise program may be as beneficial for coronary heart disease and Type 2 diabetes as frequently prescribed medications.

The Health Benefits of Exercise

1. Becoming and staying physically active can improve overall physical and psychological health.
2. Physical activity can boost energy and creativity.
3. It can help maintain independence.
4. It can help prevent or delay illness and disability.
5. Even those with chronic health concerns can benefit from appropriate forms of exercise. Exercise helps to manage stress and helps people of all ages cope with their emotions and feel better. The benefits of exercise are numerous.
6. Given that there are many different ways of exercising, from more rigorous running, hiking, swimming, to simply taking a regular 30-minute walk, there are no reasons why the majority of people of all ages cannot participate in a program of exercise.

RETIREMENT STRESS

The increase in life expectancy discussed throughout this book has had a significant influence on global work and retirement trends. The expansion of a healthy older adult population around the world has resulted in the expectation that an increasing number of older men and women will postpone retirement or partially retire, continuing to work part time, or taking period time off, or retiring from one occupation and starting another. Regardless of the circumstances, older adults, by desire or necessity, are continuing to work. For example, more than 70% of those over 50 are working in Sweden, Iceland, New Zealand, Switzerland, and Denmark. These percentages are lower in other countries, such as Hungary, Austria, Belgium, Italy, and Poland. Employment patterns are driven by a number of complex interrelated factors. However, economic and health factors appear to play a major role in retirement and work decisions (Costa & Di Milia, 2008). A number of European Union countries are considering increasing retirement age. Nevertheless, the majority of working men and women expect to and look forward to spending a number of healthy and happy years in retirement.

Despite the positive view of contemporary retirement, older adults who are retired are experiencing age discrimination at an unprecedented rate. The increased incidence of age discrimination can be linked to the economic concerns discussed previously. Although an increasing number of older men and women are continuing to work, there is also an accompanying increase in age discrimination in the work place. A difficult job market can lead to the perception that older workers are keeping much-needed jobs from younger workers.

This situation is not helped by changes in the administration of many companies, especially in the US where companies have cut their work force, forcing the remaining employees to increase their workloads thereby increasing burnout stress. They have used outsourcing to cut costs and increase profits. Outsourcing has also led to millions of layoffs. Many of those laid off are in their 50s and 60s and not ready for retirement. These workers now face difficult decisions about their expected plans for work and retirement. To add injury to insult, older workers are not only more likely to lose their jobs but also find it more difficult to find new employment (Atchley & Baruschi, 2004).

The U.S. Age Discrimination Employment Act (ADEA) of 1967 made it illegal to use age as a criterion for hiring or firing an employee. Despite the presence of this law, research findings suggest that age discrimination is still widespread (Atchley & Baruschi, 2004). Older men and women, especially during economic downturns, often wish to continue working. In the United States, one quarter of workers between the ages of 58 to 73 continue to work after retirement (Altschuler, 2004).

The ADEA banned mandatory retirement prior to age 70 for most occupations. Despite this law, the United States and other technologically advanced countries, such as Germany, Japan, and Sweden, have seen a drop in retirement age (Atchley & Baruschi, 2004). Most people expect to be able to choose the timing of their retirement. Even so, as the case of Eleanor illustrates, financial concerns during times of economic uncertainty have compelled many older adults to postpone their retirement.

The case of Eleanor

Eleanor is in her early 60s. After having taught at a high school for thirty years, she had hoped to retire and write. She lives in a large suburban house, which she and her husband purchased when their three children were small. Like many professionals, they waited to complete their education before having children. Now that their third child has finally finished school, Eleanor and her husband Karl began to plan their retirement.

In order to retire, she and Karl would have to sell their home and downsize. On a fixed income, they could not afford the mortgage payment on the spacious house they bought to raise three children. They had planned to use the equity in their house to pay cash for a smaller house. In this way, they would avoid mortgage payments. As they made their plans, they nervously watched the decline in housing prices but were shocked when they found out that their house was now worth almost one-third less than they had anticipated. Given these financial realities, they realized that they would not be able to buy a smaller place with the equity of their house. In addition, they understood that if they retired, they would not be able to continue making mortgage payments. Like many other older men and women, Eleanor had to postpone her retirement plans for a more few years.

WHAT IS RETIREMENT?

Retirement is defined as withdrawal from full-time participation in the work force.

1. Until this century, retirement was only for the rich. Everyone else worked as long as they could.
2. In 1900, the average person lived only a few years past retirement age. By 2010, if a person retired at 65, they could expect to live an average of 14 years in retirement.
3. Social Security, Medicare, and other retirement benefits have also made it possible to retire at a younger age. Changes in laws have also made it possible for elders to continue working past the age of 65. Very few occupations have a mandatory retirement age.
4. Retirement is a process that begins as soon as one thinks about what life will be like after employment.
5. Retirement involves a change in almost every aspect of life.
6. Previous experiences with life transitions will influence how changes related to retirement are confronted.
7. People usually retire by choice.
8. The decision to retire is a very personal one.
9. The most important consideration is often projected income.
10. People with rewarding jobs do not look forward to retirement as much as people in unrewarding jobs (blue-collar workers often desire retirement earlier than professional people).

One major stressor related to retirement is the feeling that one is no long useful or productive.

The transition from the world of work to retirement is a process that has gains and losses:

+ Some losses are occupational identity, daily structure of time, relationships with coworkers, work-related activities, and prestige.
+ Gains include increased time for leisure activities, travel, creative endeavors or hobbies, time for relationships, the opportunity to promote health and well-being through increased physical and social activities.

AN AGING WORLD AND RETIREMENT

The world is aging. People are living longer and healthier lives. As the older adult population continues to increase, the presence of a large population retirees can result in dramatic social and cultural change. In the United States alone, by the year 2050, it is expected one in every five people will be over the age of 65. This shift will constitute the largest percentage of retired people in history (United States Census Bureau). In the European Union, this percentage of retirees is even higher — 16.3 % of the population at present.

The Baby Boomers have already and will continue to shape the dimensions of retirement. In the United States, there are 70 million "Baby Boomers" who are expected to reach the traditional "retirement age" of 65 during the next twenty years. This demographic transformation has already begun to impact every aspect of society including the availability of Social Security benefits, the nature of health care benefits, the degree of senior housing, the texture of family relationships, and the presence of recreational programs and activities. The impact of the Baby Boomers has also shifted expectations and attitudes about retirement.

CULTURE AND VIEWS OF RETIREMENT

Cultural values shape views of retirement. In industrialized societies, people are expected to work at a factory or corporation a certain number of hours, days, and years, then retire and leave the place of their employment. This work-cycle scenario is still relatively recent. In the past, most societies were agricultural. Agricultural work on the farm did not stop on a certain day or year. Even in contemporary times, many men and women still live and work on farms. For them, like Joanna, retirement may not have any relevance or meaning.

The case of Joanna

Joanna is in her late 60s. She is a healthy and attractive woman who has spent her entire life living and working on the small family farm inherited from her parents. Johanna's husband, a contractor, worked in construction for many years and retired five years ago. In addition to a monthly Social Security check, he receives a pension from his former employer. Because Joanna has always worked on her small farm, the notion of retirement does not make sense to her. She loves her work. Although she has reached retirement age, her two cows still need to be milked, the chickens still need to be fed, and her garden still needs to be weeded. She has no pension from an employer and no Social Security. What she does have is a love of her farm and a desire to work as long as she is able.

The case of Joanna illustrates how old age and retirement have been viewed. In the past, many people lived and worked on family farms. Until the Age of Industrialization, they did not work in offices or factories. Indeed, they labored on their farms until they were no longer able to do so. When they got old, their children or grandchildren took over, working the farm and taking care of the elders. This system is no longer viable. People are not necessarily living near their families, they are living longer lives, and not everyone is like Joanna and wants to keep working. Until the 20th century, retirement was something available only for the very rich. Everyone else, like Joanna, had to work as long as they could.

The economic and social forces of globalization also present many challenges to the retirement process. Most views of retirement are based on experience in more industrialized societies (Luborsky & LeBlanc, 2003). In such societies, there is a direct relationship between age and retirement. But retirement is not synonymous with old age. From this perspective, retirement can be considered a socially acceptable removal of oneself from the workplace. In the West, there is a bureaucratic structure associated with retirement. The passage of the Social Security Act in 1935, for example, made it possible for older men and women to have a minimally sustainable income when they were no longer able to work. Social Security provided a wide range of programs, unemployment insurance, old-age assistance, aid to dependent children, and so forth making it possible for older out-of-work adults to survive in difficult times.

Although most societies provide care for older men and women, the concept of retirement is still relatively new. As the case of Joanna indicates, formal retirement in agricultural societies was not a consideration or possibility. Industrialization, demographic transformations, improved health care, and increased life expectancy have contributed to our current views and policies on retirement. Indeed, when Social Security benefits made it possible for older Americans to "retire" from full-time employment with a minimally sustainable income, the modern notion of retirement was born.

The United States was certainly not the first Western country to provide benefits for older adults. In fact, most countries in Western Europe make programs available to older adults that are more comprehensive programs than those offered in the US. Germany, for example, has long provided a thorough social service program for its older citizens. They were the first country to introduce a system of universal health care that complemented an old age pension.

Current debates over the viability of Social Security for future retirees are controversial issues and concerns regarding care for a large aging US and European population. Financial concerns often shape social attitudes toward retirement. Worries over the cost of health care, inflation and so forth, trigger considerable stress for those planning to retire (Tahmaseb-McConatha, Volkwein, Schnell, Leach, & Riley, 2003).

Demographic trends also generate concerns about modern retirement. In technologically advanced societies, such as the United States and Germany, there is a steep decline in birth rates. Present fertility rates in the US stand at 2.1 for the average number of children born per woman. In the European Union, fertility rates are at 1.5 children born for each woman. In Germany, rates are even lower. By the year 2040, in Germany there are expected to be 56 people over the age of 65 for every 100 people between the ages of 20 to 64 (Costa & Di Milia, 2008).

There is already a shortage of qualified workers in Germany. BMW, the luxury German car manufacturer, recently created a plan to make the workplace more age-friendly to meet the needs of older workers. BMW hopes that this restructuring will convince skilled workers, who are in short supply, to postpone retirement. Here's what BMW has done to make the workplace more age-friendly. They have hired physical trainers on the factory floor in order to help older workers, who do vigorous work, to stretch and exercise. They also supply ergonomic chairs, expansive exercise rooms, and other accommodations that could benefit aging workers.

It is expected that in the next 10 years almost half of BMW's 18,000 workers will be over the age of 50. Should all these workers decide to retire, would the car manufacturers be faced with a serious problem? In all, BMW's "Today for Tomorrow" project led to 70 changes. In addition to the aforementioned workplace accommodations, they have laid new floors, outfitted workers with special shoes, installed easier-to-read computer screens, established a policy to let laborers sit instead of stand, and have piped in more daylight. Other manufacturers could learn from BMW's initiative to help retain older workers who are not ready to retire. In the past five years, BMW has implemented similar ideas not only in most of its German factories, but on its assembly lines around the world (de Pommereau, 2012).

Although the decision to continue working or to retire varies, the specter of ageism has a constant negative impact on the working life of older adults. Discussed earlier in this work, ageism or age discrimination is a factor that shapes the conditions of work life for older workers in the United States and around the world. As the population of elders grows and resources diminish there is likely to be an increase in incidents of ageism — especially as politicians become increasingly concerned about the costs of health care and benefits for elders.

In response to these financial concerns, the US Congress, in 2002, raised the age eligibility for full retirement benefits from 65 to 67. These changes, which are not unique to the United States, are unpopular. Surveys in the United States and other countries indicate that only a small percentage of people are in favor of reducing benefits for older men and women. Most people stated that they preferred an expansion rather than a reduction of services.

The quality of post-retirement life is clearly based on having enough money to live comfortably. Although financial worries are a primary stressor for Americans of all ages, these concerns increase with age. Indeed, more than 17% of older Americans over the age of 65 live at or below the poverty level, with as many as 34% living just above the poverty level (United States Census Bureau).

WHAT SHALL I DO WITH MY TIME DURING RETIREMENT?

In exchange for industriousness, self-discipline and hard work, the Protestant work ethic, discussed in earlier chapters, promotes a sense of self-worth. In an era of a global work force, this ethic may no longer be viable. Consider that in some societies, the worth of the individual is not based upon her or his work ethic. Clearly there is a cultural component associated with retirement that shapes how older men and women consider their withdrawal from the work force.

The case of Ali

Ali is a respected physician in his 50s. He works long hours and loves his work. When he was a child, his family immigrated to the United States. Throughout his life, Ali's family stressed the importance of education, financial success, and making a contribution to society. His family also believes in the importance of rest, relaxation, vacations, and family commitments. They feel that these family-centered commitments are more important than work obligations. Ali agrees with his family and feels that there is more to life than work. But his sense of obligation to his calling puts a great deal of pressure on him to work long days and sometimes postpone vacations. Instead of taking notice of his dedication, Ali's family feels that he lacks the wherewithal to balance his life. Although not yet ready for retirement, Ali is beginning to think that only retirement will give him the opportunity to spend time with his aging parents, wife, and teenaged children.

The transition to retirement represents a new life stage that can bring with it the prospect of later life growth and development (Roesenkoetter & Garris, 2001). This prospect is especially true for people who have interests and involvements outside of work or those who are retiring from a stressful and unpleasant job. For these individuals, the retirement transition can be a positive long-awaited experience — a relief from the ongoing strains and conflicts of the working world.

Most people expect to retire when they are ready. Studies of retirement, as already mentioned, have pointed out that education, awareness, and planning for retirement is an important factor in making a positive adjustment to later life. As stated earlier in this chapter, an unexpected or unplanned retirement can result in considerable stress. An analysis of labor statistics indicates that up to 40% of Americans are "forced" into retirement for a variety of reasons, both personal and professional (Quinn, 2005). People may be forced to retire to due health, relationships, caregiving, or other reasons.

The Case of Ginny

Ginny worked as an administrative assistant at a university. She was 60 years old and had begun to contemplate retirement. Suddenly, her mother had a stroke and needed considerable care and support. Because Ginny was part of a small family, it would be difficult to rely on family members for social support. Her mother had no siblings, her father was dead, and her brother lived across the country. Ginny loved her mother, and they had always been close, but she was concerned about being a primary care giver. After some consideration, Ginny decided that she would take early retirement to care for her mother during her final years.

Ginny's case in not unusual. Many middle-aged adults are providing primary care for aging parents. These women and men are sometimes called the "Sandwich Generation." As they provide for their aging parents, they must also manage their own lives, work and help their children and grandchildren. Their plans for retirement may end up being based on the needs of others.

PLAN, PLAN, PLAN

Although unexpected life circumstances can lead to changes in retirement plans, planning is still an important consideration. Planning can be stressful if it leads to rumination about negative possibilities (Kraaij, Prymboom, & Ganefski, 2002; Pinquart & Sörensen, 2002). Such negative rumination was found among retirees anxious about leaving the productive world of work and how that essential separation would trigger significant life changes (Chase, Eklund & Pearson, 2003).

A carefully planned retirement appears to be a key ingredient in the recipe for a positive and productive older adulthood. Planning is particularly important for older adults who are "at risk." These are people who have serious health concerns and may need long term care or live at or near the poverty level.

Many older adults avoid planning because they
1.   May fear an uncertain future
2.   Fear a loss of independence
3.   Fear no longer being useful
4.   Have health concerns
5.   Fear being dependent on family

Planning for retirement is one way of confronting these fears and gaining a measure of control over one's life circumstances. Realistic expectations are also an important consideration for a successful retirement transition. Regardless of planning, sudden negative life events may cause those expectations to fall short. Learning how to better cope with life's unexpected twists and turns can serve as a buffer during difficult times. When planning, it is important to realize that priorities and activities in pre-retirement will continue to be of interest and will influence post-retirement time.

TIMING AND RETIREMENT

Timing is a critical factor associated with a successful transition to retirement. Retirees are likely to feel unsettled or stressed if they believe they have been forced to retire earlier than is socially acceptable. In the US, the age of 65 tends to be norm for retirement. The "right" time to retire is when it "feels" right. This varies for each person. In some cases, there is a decline in work ability (Costa & Sartori, 2007). Decline depends on the type of work. Clearly, heavy blue-collar jobs become more difficult with age. With age it becomes increasingly important to have a compatible "fit" between the skills and interests of the individual and the job. The retirement experience is shaped by multiple intersecting influences.

GENDER AND RETIREMENT

Men and women may not share similar work and retirement experiences. Gender can define the meaning of work and retirement. In 2012, women accounted for 47% of the workforce in the United States. Seventy-two million women (58% of all women) in the United States worked full or part-time. On average, women still appeared to work in lower status occupations and earned 81 cents for every dollar earned by American men.

These inequalities have dogged women throughout their work lives. They have also shaped their retirement experiences. Recent studies have found that as women age, they may wish to or need to continue working. Even so, they experience a greater degree of age discrimination than older male workers. Older women who continue to work are often under-employed, a situation in which their talents are not recognized or their salaries are not on a par with their qualifications. A recent study of women aged 55 to 61 found that many were underemployed and that the pay gap between men and women tended to increase with age. Frustrations such as these can result in an early retirement decision, perhaps before one is ready (Stark, 2012).

When it comes to successful retirement planning and preparation, ageism and gender discrimination combine to place women at a significant disadvantage. A persistent lack of resources for retirement, lower monthly Social Security and private pension payments, may require women of retirement age to continue in the labor force. The feminist movement of the 1970s, which contemporary older workers experienced, has affected their views on education and occupation. These same older workers may have also experienced material deprivation and racist policies that may contribute to their concerns about remaining in the work force, a decision that would maintain their income and independence (Altschuler, 2004).

Gender-related stress among older females is associated with caregiving. Women are still responsible for the majority of familial caregiving and are responsible for the bulk of household chores. When women retire, these domestic responsibilities do not change. Despite the domestic difficulties, women do have an advantage over retired men. Unlike most men, women take advantage of social and emotional support systems. While men have a larger network of acquaintances, women have more contact with and support from their friends, family, and acquaintances. These relationships make it a bit easier for women to cope with stressors associated with aging and retirement. The connection among stress, relationships, and social support will be discussed in more detail in the next chapter.

When one leaves the life of work in which people establish networks of social relationships, what happens to the retiree's social life? Retired women tend to have extensive social contacts outside the world of work. Women tend to confide in other women. For their emotional intimacy, men tend to rely on their spouse. Even when women become widowed or divorced, they are better able to develop and sustain new relationships.

Loneliness, then, is a concern for retired men who no longer have the structure of work and relationships with co-workers to shape their social lives. Retirement for men who had high-status occupations is particularly stressful. During retirement, they often become lonely and suffer from significant status loss. As previously mentioned, retired men lose many of their social contacts. For these reasons, men are especially vulnerable to the negative effects of retirement and aging.

The case of Jason

Jason is in his late 70s, and is an oncologist who loves his work. He still works three days a week. He feels that his life has a good balance of home and work. His partner, who is in his early 60s, manages Jason's office and decides to retire early. This decision forces Jason into retirement. Although he enjoys doing research, tending his garden, and writing essays, Jason misses his patients and his friends at work. Six months after retiring Jason became seriously depressed. Luckily Jason's wife intervened. She insisted that Jason seek help. She also got him involved in community affairs, as well as part time consulting. Once he felt better, Jason realized that he needed to keep busy. Each day he made sure to engage in at least one commitment. Jason is lucky that his wife compelled him to seek help. Not everyone is so lucky!

WHO AM I NOW?

Retirement involves a change in identity. It is a social identity that is shaped by the loss of an important life role — someone who works. As mentioned earlier, the more invested someone is in his or her job, the more likely she or he will to want to continue working.

If the role of worker has been central to one's identity, as in Jason's case, its loss may be an especially stressful concern. A positive transition to retirement devolves from a sense of continuity between "retirement me" and one's previous work identity. We have already stressed how important planning is to the successful retirement process, but retirement planning also requires a measure of self-understanding as well as willingness for creative self-exploration.

In order for retirement to fulfill one's plans and goals for the "golden years," one should take into account interests and activities that have been pleasurable and meaningful earlier in life (McConatha, Reiser-Danner, McConatha, Hayta, & Polat, 2004; McConatha, Volkwein, Schnell, Leach, & Riley, 2003). It is important to remember that every change in life is associated with stress and anxiety.

Even so there have been transformations in the scope and texture of social life for older adults. Changes in lifestyle, improved health care, and increased life expectancy have resulted in a growing number of older adults who have challenged the traditional images of old age as a time of decline and ill health. These images reinforce societal attitudes that "old age," the retirement years, is something to be avoided and feared. Indeed, fear and anxiety about the aging process can cause people to feel anxious or depressed about making the transition to retirement. Retirement-related stressors, like loss of status, financial restrictions, and health concerns, may compound this fear and anxiety (Kraaij, Prymboom, & Ganefski, 2002).

A HAPPY RETIREMENT

Despite the issues previously outlined, the majority of older adults make a positive adjustment to retirement (Chase, Eklund and Pearson, 2003). If older adults receive a satisfactory income, possess good health, like their relationships, and enjoy recreational interests, they are likely to be happy during retirement. Adequate coping skills are helpful in dealing with any life transition, especially later life transitions. Discussed in Chapter 1, techniques for coping with stressful transitions vary with age. Older men and women tend to engage in emotion-focused coping (e.g., distancing) as opposed to problem-focused (e.g., planning, problem-solving) coping (Folkman, Lazarus, Pimley, & Novacek, 1987).

Both forms of coping can have positive and detrimental impacts. Problem-focused coping may either be proactive/preventative (e.g., planning for retirement) or reactive (e.g., coping with retirement after being retired). Emotion-focused coping tends to be reactive only. The reduction of immediate anxiety can be a specious reinforcement for older adults to engage in one coping strategy over another (Folkman, Lazarus, Pimley & Novacek, 1987).

Research on coping has found that as one ages, he or she shifts to more mature coping mechanisms. As we age, there is increasing reliance on cognitive adjustment. Put another way, older individuals shift the focus of their attention away from limiting factors and situations. Instead, they focus on situations that are not associated with loss. This process provides greater flexibility. Indeed, the retirement years are marked by personal resilience (Hamarat, et al., 2002).

RESILIENCE AS A COPING MECHANISM DURING RETIREMENT

Positive reappraisal decreases anxiety and depression. This strategy is not a mere acceptance of a situation. Acceptance and negative rumination can increase stress and anxiety.

1. Avoid negative rumination
2. Attach positive meaning to situations
3. Focus on personal growth
4. Stay or become physically active
5. Stay socially engaged, maintain work relationships or replace them with new friendships

Positive reappraisal is becoming more and more important as the world becomes increasingly complex and interconnected. In cross-cultural studies of middle-aged and retirement-aged men and women in Germany, for example, researchers found that a positive interpretation of a situation was critical to a satisfying later life. Positive reappraisal is also associated with personal growth and satisfaction in relationships (Wrosch, Heckhausen, & Lachman, 2000).

Socio-emotional selectivity theory (Carstensen, Fung, & Charles, 2003) offers an explanation for age-related changes in coping. This theory states that older adults realize that time is limited. As a consequence, they tend to focus only on more meaningful life elements: time with family, personal fulfillment, satisfying activities.

The transition from work to retirement is, of course, an important milestone. Coping strategies can help make the retirement transition a positive one. Pearlin and Schooler (1978) discussed three coping strategies:

1. Changing the situation (e.g., negotiate, seek advice, etc.)
2. Changing personal interpretation (e.g., positive reappraisal, humor, faith, etc.)
3. Managing emotion (e.g., exercise, therapy, relaxation, etc.)

It is important to have skills in all these areas, but as discussed in later life changing personal interpretation can take on a more significant role.

Not only that, but it takes time to make a positive adjustment. There appear to be phases to the retirement process that are common for a majority of retirees. They follow in sequential order:

PHASES IN RETIREMENT

1. Honeymoon
2. Disenchantment
3. Acceptance
4. Realistic reappraisal

Retirement is an important later life transition that presents challenges and opportunities for older men and women. This chapter has demonstrated that there is no one clear picture of retirement. As the workforce in technologically advanced societies such as the United States becomes increasingly diverse, the picture of retirement is likely to become even more complex. The case of William Miller below reflects the increasingly diverse picture of retirement.

William Miller, a short muscular 80-year-old African-American man looks down at his thick, ashy hands — evidence of years of hard manual work as he tells the story of his life. Miller loves to tell stories, especially stores about his own and his family's experiences. He enjoys talking about how time has changed the way of life he knew as a young man. Although his 80 years have been filled with hardship, he is a very positive person. He often follows statements about the difficult challenges in his life with: „but, you know, things were good." Miller's strength comes from his faith, his church, and his family. He has experienced years of racial discrimination and prejudice, but he says that his faith helped him forgive and forget.

Even though Miller is "retired," he nonetheless spends his mornings as the maintenance supervisor of a large historic apartment building. He accepted this position more than 20 years ago after he "retired" from a job he had worked for more than 30 years. For 18 years, Miller worked Monday through Friday from seven in the morning until early afternoon. Even on Sundays he would come in before church in order to check on potential problems. When he began to suffer from back and leg problems and was diagnosed with gout, he decided it was time to really retire. He was given a retirement party and small bonus. After six months he felt better, but unfortunately he also found that he needed to return to work. Without the income from his part-time job, he was unable to pay his and his wife's monthly medication bills, which exceed $200 a month. The residents of the building where he still works were very grateful for Miller's return; he is perhaps the only person who is capable of dealing with the many problems in the old building. Indeed, Miller prides himself on his ability to fix the multiple problems that arise on a regular basis. Although he is pleased to have people compliment him on his skills, he wishes he did not have to depend on this job and income during his "retirement" years. He would love to be able to drop in when needed in order to "troubleshoot" instead of having to make his way to work every day.

William Miller presents one picture of contemporary retirement. It is not the image that mainstream Americans have of a typical retired person enjoying a carefree life of leisure. William Miller presents a portrait in "a different shade of gray," a portrait that is becoming more common (Newman, 2003). There is no one "face of retirement" in the 21st century. Each scenario is associated with stressors and satisfactions. As the number of full and part-time "retirees" increases, it is important to address the ways in which these men and women can cope with transitional stress associated with retirement. This chapter has touched on contemporary retirement trends, concerns of those who are contemplating retirement, and thoughts for coping with the transition to retirement.

REFERENCES

+ Atchley, R.C., & Barusch, A.S. *Social Forces and Aging: An Introduction to Social Gerontology* (10th Ed.). Belmont, CA: Wadsworth/Thomson Learning.

+ Altschuler, J. (2004). Beyond money and survival: The meaning of paid work among older women. *International Journal of Aging and Human Development, 58*(3), 223-239.

+ Carstensen, L., Fung, H., & Charles, S. (2003). Socioemotional selectivity theory and the regulation of emotion in the second half of life. *Motivation and Emotion, 27*(2), 103-123.

+ Chase, C. I., Eklund, S. J., & Pearson, L. M. (2003). Affective responses of faculty emeriti to retirement. *Educational Gerontology, 29*, 521-534

+ Costa, G. & Di Mili, L. (2008) Aging and shift work: A complex problem to face. *Chronobiology International, 25*(2&3), 165-181.

+ Costa, G. & Sartori, S. (2007). Ageing, working hours, and workability. *Ergonomics, 50*: 1-17.

+ de Pommereau, I. (2012 September 2) *How BMW reinvents the factory for older workers.* Retrieved on September 28, 2013 from http://www.csmonitor.com/World/Europe/2012/0902/How-BMW-reinvents-the-factory-for-older-workers

+ Exercise as Preventive Medicine. (2013, October 15). *New York Times*, D6.

+ Folkman, S., Lazarus, R.S., Pimley, S., & Novacek, J. (1987). Age differences in stress and coping processes. *Psychology and Aging, 2*(2), 171-184.

+ Hamarat, E., Thompson, D., Steele, D., Matheny, K., & Simons, C. (2002). Age differences in coping resources and satisfaction with life among middle-aged, young-old, and oldest-old adults. *Journal of Geriatric Psychology, 163*(3), 360-367.

+ Kraaij, V., Pruymboom, E., & Garnefski, N. (2002). Cognitive coping and depressive symptoms in the elderly: A longitudinal study. *Aging & Mental Health, 6*(3), 275-281.

+ Luborsky, M.R., & LeBlanc, I.M. (2003). Cross-cultural perspectives on the concept of retirement: An analytic redefinition. *Journal of Cross-Cultural Gerontology, 18*, 251-271.

+ McConatha, J. Tahmaseb, Rieser-Danner, L., McConatha, P.D., Hayta, V., & Polat, T. S. (2004) A comparative analysis of Turkish and US attitudes toward aging. *The Journal of Educational Gerontology, 30*(3), 169-183.

+ McConatha, J. Tahmaseb & Volkwein, K. (2012) *The Social Geography of Aging.* Oxford, England: Meyer & Meyer.

+ McConatha, J. Tahmaseb, Volkwein, K., Schnell, F., Leach, E., & Riley, L. (2003) Attitudes toward aging: A comparative analysis of young adults from the United States and Germany. *The International Journal of Aging and Human Development, 57*(3), 203-215.

+ Newman, K.S. (2003). *A Different Shade of Grey: Midlife and Beyond in the Inner City.* New York: The New Press.

+ Pearlin, L. I., & Schooler, C. (1978). The structure of coping. *Journal of Health and Social Behavior, 19*, 2-21.

+ Pinquart, M., & Sörensen, S. (2002). Factors that promote and prevent preparation for future care needs: Perceptions of older Canadian, German, and US women. *Health Care for Women International, 23*, 729-741.

+ Quinn, J.B. (2005, February 14). Your retirement: How to land on your feet. *Newsweek, 145*, 47-52.

+ Roesenkoetter, M. M., & Garris, J.M. (2001). Retirement planning, use of time, and psychosocial adjustment. *Issues in Mental Health Nursing, 22*, 703-722.

+ Stark, L. (2012 May 2012). *Older women kicked to the curb, report finds.* Retrieved September 13, 2013 from http://abcnews.go.com/blogs/business/2012/05/older-working-women-kicked-to-curb-report-finds/

+ United States Census Bureau (n.d.). Retrieved (October 10, 2013) from www.census.gov.

+ Wrosch, C., Heckhaussen, J., & Lachman, M. E. (2000). Primary and secondary control strategies for managing health and financial stress across adulthood. *Psychology and Aging, 15*(3), 387-399.

CHAPTER FOUR

Relationships, Social Support and Coping with Stress

CHAPTER FOUR

Relationships, Social Support and Coping with Stress

Oh, I get by with a little help from my friends
Mmm, I get high with a little help from my friends
Mmm, gonna try with a little help from my friends
What do I do when my love is away
Does it worry you to be alone?
How do I feel by the end of the day
Are you sad because you're on your own?

The above lyrics from the Beatles' Sergeant Pepper's Lonely Hearts Club Band album (1967) emphasize the power of relationships. People are social animals. They need each other in order to survive and thrive. What people need changes over their lifespan, but people of all ages need to give and receive support and affirmation from others.

Middle and later adulthood presents unique challenges for the development and maintenance of satisfying relationships. In this chapter, I will discuss theories and research related to some of ways that relationships and social support can help older women and men manage and cope with life stress. It is impossible to discuss all aspects of social relationships so I have chosen theories and research that provide a broad view of this important life dimension.

Relationships vary across the adult lifespan. What we need to be happy at one part in our lives is going to change as our roles and expectations change. The one constant is that we continue to need people. We need friends, we need family, and we need a community of support. Some people only need one or two people while others may need a larger network. There is no correct number as long as one is satisfied and one has support during difficult times. This chapter addresses research focusing on relationship between stress, happiness, health, and relationships. I will also provide some practical suggestions for combating the potentially devastating effects of loneliness and social isolation.

Developing and maintaining positive and satisfying relationships requires hard work, dedication, and sacrifice. Modern life is filled with more opportunities and challenges than ever before in history. People move from place to place, live far from their families, are able to connect with potential partners in any part of the world through the internet, and make new friends or connect with old friends via Facebook, email, and text. By the same token, studies show that loneliness and isolation are on the increase. The availability of so many opportunities can also increase stress and anxiety. The overabundance of choice can make us question ourselves and our relationships. Are they satisfying and fulfilling? Are there more satisfying and fulfilling relationships elsewhere? Should we work so hard at our relationships or search elsewhere for easier, potentially better ones?

LONELINESS AND ISOLATION

Research shows that despite the many ways that we can connect with others, loneliness and feelings of isolation are actually increasing. Loneliness and social isolation present risks to psychological and physical health. Loneliness is a complex, unpleasant feeling associated with a lack of satisfying connections. It can lead to health concerns and dissatisfaction with life. Loneliness is experienced when there are no available satisfying social connections. Social isolation relates to feeling disconnected from the community or society in which one lives. Feelings of isolation may increase with age, especially if age is accompanied by a decline in health, a change in residence, or the inability to keep up with rapid technological changes.

Although everyone is lonely some of the time, some people experience chronic loneliness. The core concept of loneliness and social isolation are deprivation of social connections. Such depravation leads to feelings of abandonment, a lack of intimate attachments, and even feelings of emptiness. Loneliness and social isolation destroy health and happiness; they can even lead to premature death. Being lonely and/or isolated can lead to anxiety, depression, and lowered self-esteem and self-conception. People feel that they are a failure as a person because they cannot make satisfactory connections with others. The case of Gerri illustrates how we are all potentially at risk for feeling lonely and isolated.

Gerri is an attractive outgoing woman in her 60s. She works part-time as a book editor. Two years ago Gerri fell during a biking trip and injured her knee. The pain made her unable to bike and hike, two of her favorite activities. As a result she lost touch with several of the women she used to socialize with. Since she lives alone, she began to feel lonely and anxious about going out. As a result she reduced her activities even more. After several months, her knee had healed, yet Gerri seemed unable to go back to her usual activities. She now rarely socialized. If she did not have to go to work, she tended to stay home. She felt listless and down much of the time.

Luckily Gerri realized she had allowed herself to become lonely and isolated from her friends. Gerri knew she needed to reach out to someone. She called one of her friends with whom she used to hike. Although it was hard for her, Gerri explained what was going on, and her friend immediately offered help and encouragement. Gerri's friend kindly agreed to pick her up each week for their regular hike and lunch, and encouraged Gerri to join other activities. After a few weeks Gerri felt much better, she went out more, reconnected with some of her friends, and felt much happier.

Gerri's situation was more likely to occur because she lived alone. A recent Los Angeles Times article stated that people living alone make up 27% of American households. This is a dramatic increase from previous decades. The reasons this solo living occurs include later marriages, fewer children, and a longer life expectancy. The number of older adults living alone also has increased, by choice and by necessity (Alpert, 2013).

Although more Americans are opting to live alone, contemporary social factors influence loneliness. Social mobility, immigration, and migration all influence the availability of family and kin. Technological advancements mentioned earlier make connection easier, but they can also lead to increases in feelings of isolation and alienation. The risk of isolation increases with age, especially if aging is accompanied by decreased mobility, a decline in health, and increased impairment. Social science research and theories focusing on basic human needs have demonstrated that our need for others comes just after basic needs such as food and shelter.

HUMANISTIC PSYCHOLOGY AND RELATIONSHIPS

Humanistic psychologists focus on what makes people healthy and happy. These psychologists believe that each person is unique and able to fulfill their individual potential if his or her needs are met. A very important component of human need is the need to connect with others and have satisfying relationships that lead to self-esteem, affirmation, and self-actualization.

According to humanistic theorist Abraham Maslow, relationships and social connections have been placed directly above basic survival needs such as food and shelter (Maslow, 1968). Maslow was one of the first psychologists to study the motivations of "healthy" people. He focused on deficiency needs and growth needs. Maslow presented a hierarchy of human needs, described below. His hierarchy included basic human needs such as food, shelter, and safety. Human relationships follow directly after these basic human needs. In other words, we need people to survive.

The model above proposed by psychologist Maslow illustrates basic needs, as well as growth needs culminating in self-actualization. Once lower level needs have been somewhat satisfied, a person can move on to growth needs. It is not possible to move on to self-actualization or self-esteem without satisfying connections with others. Given that relationships are essential to overall well-being, the increase in loneliness in the contemporary world presents a crisis threatening global health and happiness.

In one study in England ("Loneliness Research", 2013), researchers found:

+ Between 6% and 13% of people aged over 65 say they feel always or very lonely
+ 17% of older people are in contact with family, friends and neighbors less than once a week and 11% are in contact less than once a month
+ Over half (51%) of all people age 75 and over live alone
+ Half of all older people (about 5 million) say the television is their main company
+ 63% of adults age 52 or over who have been widowed, and 51% of the same group who are separated or divorced report, feeling lonely some of the time or often
+ 59% of adults over age 52 who report poor health say they feel lonely some of the time or often
+ A higher percentage of women than men report feeling lonely.

This information is similar to statistics from the United States and other Western countries. Clearly loneliness and isolation presents a serious threat to overall well-being. Research indicates that social isolation increases the risk for all causes of death, including heart disease, cancer, stroke, accidents, or suicide (Taylor, 2002). Psychological distress increases when social support is lacking.

Robert D. Putnam, in his book *Bowling Alone* published in 2000, states that civil society is breaking down in the United Sates. He believes that people are becoming increasingly disconnected from their families and communities. Using the analogy of the bowling league, Putman discussed the decline of community activities and an increase in alienation and isolation. Is it true that people in our contemporary world live increasingly isolated lives? If this is the case, does the problem increase with age and possibly cause a decline in health? If connections are necessary for our basic survival, what factors lead to an increase in satisfying human relationships?

WHAT ARE SOCIAL NETWORKS?

One of the ways of maintaining a sense of social connection and integration is through the establishment of social support networks. Social support networks serve the function of meeting instrumental and emotional support needs (Antonucci & Akiyama, 1991). Social networks consist of relatives, friends, and neighbors, who surround a person in a mutually beneficial network.

Social supports are based on social exchange and reciprocity. The more equitable a relationship is the more satisfying it tends to be. In fact, equity theory, proposed by psychologist John S. Adams (1963), focuses on the importance of a balance of input and output in order to maintain satisfaction with a relationship. The theory is based on the notion of fair treatment in the workplace and can be applied to personal relationships. As the case of Walter and Sam below illustrates, equity is subjective.

Walter and Sam have been friends for many years. They met in college more than 30 years ago. Sam who is quiet and shy was drawn to Walter's gregariousness. Walter enjoyed Sam's ability to listen intently and make insightful suggestions. They formed a lifelong friendship. To the casual observer, they might appear strange. Walter is constantly talking animatedly while Sam quietly listens. Some people believe that Walter takes advantage of Sam. But Sam and Walter are both content and satisfied with the relationship. Walter helps Sam be more social, Sam helps Walter pause and think about his choices. They enjoy and value their friendship.

PEOPLE WHO NEED PEOPLE

Friends and family provide us with help and support. Numerous studies have shown that satisfying relationships are associated with better health and greater happiness. Relationships and social support serve as an intervening variable that mediates life stress. Satisfying relationships serve as a buffer during stressful negative life events. Social support can come from family, friends, romantic partners, pets, community ties, and coworkers. The nature of the support depends on the needs of the person. Attachment, intimacy, social integration, opportunity for nurturing, reassurance, support, and help are all important aspects of social support provided by relationships that work.

Relationships are complex. What one person finds interesting and satisfying, another person finds stressful and irritating. Some of us need many people in our lives, we need to socialize on a regular basis, have someone to talk to on a daily basis. For others, occasional socializing and having one friend or family member who is available to them is sufficient. There is no right or wrong way to have healthy relationships.

Erin and Karin are sisters. Both are in their late 50s. Erin works at home as an accountant. She is unmarried and spends her days in her study working for a carpet cleaning company. She enjoys her work and likes living alone. On Wednesday evenings she goes swimming and then has dinner with Karin and two old friends from school. They listen to each other and chat about their concerns. On the weekend Erin usually goes out with a male companion she has been seeing for two years. He lives two hours away and usually drives over on Saturdays and spends the night driving back Sunday mid-day. Erin is happy to live alone and finds the solitude of her life satisfying.

Karin is married with three grown children and two grandchildren. She works as a nurse, has many friends in her neighborhood and with is friendly with her co-workers. Karin goes out almost every night. She and her husband visit one of their children, or they eat out with friends, or they barbeque. Karin is busy and happy to be busy and socially active.

The case of Karin and Erin illustrates the differences in what people find satisfying. Expectations about relationships vary by individual personality, social class, age, gender, and culture.

THEORIES OF RELATIONSHIPS

Social scientists have constructed theories that help explain the importance of social relationships across lifespans. The convoy model of social support (Kahn & Antonucci, 1980) is one important theory that is useful in understanding how our needs for connections and people change over time. This theory illustrates that support is always important but that the specific aspect of support changes with age and life circumstances. This theory is depicted in three concentric circles each describing the source of support from which people construct their networks (Kahn & Antonucci, 1980). Circles are used to demonstrate the importance and closeness of some relationships. Antonucci, Akiyama, and Takahashi (2004) provide examples of how a person's convoy changes with age and development. The model below is provides an example on a convoy.

The convoy model emphasizes that the people one may consider crucial during one's teens are not likely to be the same people one has in one's inner circle at 50 or at 70. Those people may remain important but not as central. The theory is a useful tool for evaluating the importance of particular relationships (Kahn & Antonucci, 1980). The inner circle includes intimate family and friends. The outer two circles consist of other important systems of support, support that is important but not essential to emotional well-being. With life changes, the make-up of the circles also changes.

The Conservation of Resources theory (COR) is another useful theory that emphasized the importance of relationships to one's ability to cope with life stress. This theory describes people's desire to develop and conserve personal and social resources (Hobfoll, Freedy, Lane, & Geller, 1990). This model of social support explains that people need to rely on their social resources and relationships in difficult stressful times. If we have social relationships in the form of family and friends, we are more likely to have the resources to cope with stressful life events.

The Conservation of Resources Theory (COR) focuses on our desire to preserve and protect what is important to us. Our relationships and social support help us feel good about ourselves, develops our self-esteem, and helps us feel more in control of our lives.

1.   Our friends and family validate who we are.
2.   When we feel threatened, we rely on them to help us.
3.   In times of stress and loss, these resources serve as buffers.
4.   They are our building blocks for health and happiness.

It is safe to say that social support is necessary for survival. It provides a person with a sense of interpersonal connectedness, a more positive and valued sense of self, assistance in times of need, and a mechanism to help cope in stressful times.

DIMENSIONS OF SOCIAL SUPPORT

Social support has both structural and perceptual dimensions. The structural dimension of social support consists of marital status, number of friends/ family members, supportive acts provided, frequency of contact. The perceptual dimension of social support is more subjective and based on how an individual perceives his or her social support system. It includes satisfaction with support. Social relationships that are frustrating and do not provide one with needed support are damaging to well-being.

The case of Collins

Collins, in her late 60s, has a younger sister. Collins' sister has always asked her for help with her problems, which are both financial and personal. Collins is happy to help and listen, and even to lend money. However, over the years Collins has begun to feel anxious and frustrated when she and her sister get together. She feels that her sister does not really listen to her. When Collins brings up concerns, her sister listens for a moment and then dismisses Collins' concerns moving the topic to her own problems. While this is a long-standing pattern, in recent years it has begun to make Collins dissatisfied and frustrated with her relationship with her sister. She now sees her less often and spends more of her free time with her friends. She is sad about the change in her relationship with her sister but feels that it is for the best. It is hard to always give and not receive in return.

According to psychological research, relationship satisfaction is based on one's appraisal of the satisfaction of the relationship (Carstensen, 1992). If the relationship makes one feel loved, cared for and valued, and it is mutual then it is more likely to lead to satisfaction.

There is no one way to have a relationship. People are different; one person may only wish for and need one friend while another feels lonely if he or she does not regularly connect with several people. Whether an individual's support system is large or small does not matter, what matters is if it meets an individual's needs. As long as that need is satisfied for the person, the person is likely to be healthier and happier than someone who feels lonely and isolated. There is a negative correlated relationship between perceived social support and the severity of psychological and physical problems. In other words, the more satisfied one is, the less likely one is to be physically or psychologically distressed (Cecil, et al., 1995).

SOCIAL SUPPORT AND RELATIONSHIPS ACROSS THE LIFESPAN

Our early life relationships can shape the structure of later relationships. When we have support and love early in life, we tend to become more self-reliant and trusting. We are also better able to provide support for others. Ainsworth and Bowlby (1991), early attachment theorists and researchers, found that early relationships influence later life personality adjustment and psychological distress.

A compilation of stressful life events, adverse childhood experiences, and low levels of social support may predict maladjustment in adulthood. A child's resilience under stress increases as a result of increased family support. In adolescence, those with more family support tend to be happier and more affectionate (Bronfenbrenner, 1961).

According to attachment theories, early life attachments between children and primary care givers are primary in shaping later life relationships. Ainsworth and Bowlby's theory of attachment states that infants have a pre-programmed biological basis for becoming attached. Attachment is a survival strategy; it protects from the dangers of the environment. A parent's sensitivity to a child's needs is important in the development of different forms of attachment. Children can become attached in different ways:
1.   Securely attached: sensitive, warm, and positive
2.   Avoidant children: fear becoming close to someone
3.   Ambivalent: uncertain in their response, often based on early life inconsistent support and involvement.

These early patterns can carry into adulthood, but they do not doom one to be happy or unhappy in later life. Awareness of early life patterns and a commitment to change can result in fulfilling satisfying later life relationships.

STRESS, HEALTH, AND SOCIAL SUPPORT

Loneliness and a lack of satisfying relationships can present a threat to physical and psychological health and happiness. Research has shown that not having satisfying relationships has an equivalent risk factor for early mortality as smoking 15 cigarettes a day, and is worse for us than other well-known risk factors, such as obesity and physical inactivity. We cannot be healthy in isolation. We need the support of friends, family, and community.

Health needs to be understood from a holistic point of view. One is not "healthy" when one is not ill or in pain. A healthy person has positive feelings about life, has satisfying relationships, and he or she has the ability to manage stress. There are a number of factors that influence someone's ability to be optimally healthy. Satisfying support from relationships is a crucial component of overall health and well-being. This chapter has already addressed the importance of relationships for health and happiness. The existence of satisfying connections also serves as a key factor in the development and maintenance of living a healthy active lifestyle.

Many studies have explored the relationships between healthy lifestyles and healthy relationships. One classic study started in the 1930s at the Human Population Laboratory of the University of California Berkeley, in Alameda County, California, explored the lifestyle of residents over a long period of time. The researchers focused on factors that maintained health. Many years later they found that in addition to smoking, exercise, sleep, diet, and other factors, social ties played a strong role within the lifespan (Kaplan, Seeman, Cohen, Knudsen, & Guralnik, 1987). Social ties could take the form of marriage, family, friends, or community memberships. Making use of social ties as a coping strategy maintained and improved health. Social ties provided both emotional support and instrumental support during stressful times. Everyone finds themselves lonely at some point in life; when this occurs, it is possible to make use of this experience to make changes as a person. What can be done to combat loneliness?

1. Use loneliness as a way to grow as a person
2. Keep yourself open to new relationships and activities
3. Develop positive attitudes about yourself and others
4. Stay busy
5. Reach out to others
6. Do not be afraid to make yourself vulnerable (remember everyone has the same need to connect and feel validated)
7. Avoid negative rumination
8. Join groups and organization
9. Become physically active
10. Set goals for yourself
11. Seek the help of a professional

In an article on combating loneliness, Lisa McShane (2008) provides similar suggestions:

1. Revive dreams you've had and do something about them each day.
2. Rev up those qualities you like about yourself. Become stronger so that your weaknesses fade away.

3. Rev up your health. Eat well and exercise often to raise your body's endorphin levels.

4. Remember past love and pay no attention to old and sad stories of your life.

5. Remain as optimistic as you can and expect that good things will happen to you. Give thanks for what you are blessed with and be eager to share your blessings with others.

6. Use the Five Rs in order to fall in love with yourself all over again and others will see the radiance of your self-love. You will have learned how to deal with loneliness.

7. Since similar things attract other similar things, you are bound to attract a person who also has self-love. All of this will cure loneliness and send you on your way toward a healthy, loving relationship.

THE GENDERED NATURE OF HUMAN RELATIONSHIPS

There are gender differences in relationships. Developmental psychologists have stated that women are socialized to be more relational than men (Baker-Miller, 1976). In other words, women tend to reach out to others more than men. They are more willing to let others know that they need connections. Therefore women are more adept at relying on their friends and family during stressful times.

Women are more likely to turn to others for help. They are more likely to discuss their problems and concerns and seek help and advice. By the same token, they are also more likely to sacrifice their personal desires and wishes for those of the family or group, a situation that can increase stress.

Male socialization often inhibits the expression of concerns, fears, and stressors. Men are less likely to allow themselves to appear vulnerable. Depression research indicates that men are less likely to seek help for their depression and more likely to mask depression with alcohol (Alcoholism: Clinical & Experimental Research, 2008). Men also have a tendency to withdraw in stressful circumstances. Such withdrawal negatively impacts their health and happiness.

Although common beliefs indicate that men are able to manage their concerns and negative feelings well, some researchers have proposed that men are more physiologically reactive to stress than women, particularly in the adrenergic parts of the cardiovascular system and in the stress-related endocrine responses (Obrist, 1981). Men may experience more physiological symptoms in the face of stress, such as increased heart rate and blood pressure.

Women on the other hand are more likely to turn to others in times of stress. Such a tendency is healthy and adaptive and serves as a buffer to stressful life events. The neuroendocrine system helps explain why the ways those positive relationships can promote health (Taylor, 2002). Oxytocin, a hormone that is released during times of stress compels people to seek others, oxytocin is also released when one is hugged, touched, or feels connected to others, such exposure then promotes health and happiness (Goldsher, n.d.).

Many studies have emphasized the ways in which social support helps us cope with various stress-producing life situations. It has been found that lower perceived family support has been linked to higher levels of stress. Social support even affects the risk of mortality and heart disease (Cohen, 1988; House, Landis, & Umberson, 1988), adjustment to abortion (Major, et al., 1990), and suicide (Welz, Veiel, & Hafner, 1988).

Stressful events are more likely to cause psychiatric disorders in people who are living alone, widowed, or feel lonely and isolated. Depression is the number one mental health disorder worldwide, and depressed people often lack supportive people in their lives.

Not having access to satisfying relationships and social support leads to loneliness. Loneliness can further lead to isolation. Lonely people are less likely to be involved in activities that build social networks, such as attending religious services, volunteering, participating in a community organization or spending time on a hobby. Loneliness is therefore a factor leading to social isolation and poor health (Loneliness among older adults: A national survey of adults 45+, 2010).

Earlier in the chapter, I proposed some ways to combat loneliness. It is important to remember that there is no one way to do this. Older people are not all the same; people have different personalities and different needs regardless of age and gender. If you want to help someone combat loneliness, start with the individual. Cattan, White, Bond, & Learmouth (2005) mention 3 areas of loneliness intervention:

1. Start with individual — their interests, the type of experience they are facing: isolation or loneliness?
2. Involve each person in shaping various activities
3. Group activities often work since the group members can provide support for each other

FRIENDSHIPS

Friendships are very different from family relationships. Friends are voluntary relationships. They are chosen relationships that we may maintain or lose as we change social roles. We are happier if we have friendships, but many of our friendships may play a limited role in our lives. Our friendships are based on trust, similarity of interests, mutual attraction, and reciprocity. Friendships begin on the surface with very little emotional disclosure; as trust builds, people gradually feel more comfortable disclosing personal matters and seeking help in times of stress.

Factors that Influence and Shape Friendships

+ Personality
+ Neighborhood
+ Work and retirement
+ Similar interests
+ Health and mobility
+ Cultural differences — in more collectivist cultures people place less emphasis on friends and more on family ties

WHAT CHANGES OCCUR ACROSS THE ADULT LIFESPAN IN FRIENDSHIPS?

In early adulthood men and women tend to have a larger network of friends. People may seek intimacy with someone they do not know well. Sometimes these friendships remain, other times they may dissolve just as quickly as they were formed. By the late 20s and 30s, instant intimacy is unthinkable for people, and friendships tend to take much longer to achieve, but once achieved they tend to be more stable and enduring.

During midlife, when we are busy with work, children, spouses, when there is little time for life's necessitates and pleasures, friendships, although still important, take a back seat to other responsibilities. Middle-aged adults spend less than 10% of their time with friends. Once the children are more independent, careers are more established, there is a re-emphasis on the importance of friendship.

Like other aspects of life, later life presents challenges and pleasures when it comes to forming and maintaining friendships. Being socially integrated is helpful to longevity. Some research indicated that the larger a person's social network is the happier and healthier they are likely to be (Holt-Lunstad, Smith, & Layton, 2010). As I have previously mentioned in this chapter, this is not necessarily true for everyone. Quantity is not quality in relationships. What is important is a fit between a person's needs and his or her social network.

There are many new ways of connecting and finding friends and partners, but this chapter does not discuss these in detail. But the internet and newspapers are awash with "seeking friendship" columns and dating services, proving that many people need a hand in making new friends. It is made more difficult by our tendency to view with suspicion anyone striking up a conversation with a stranger. As we get older and accustomed to our familiar routine, we meet fewer new people, and have less drive to take the leap to initiate friendship.

GENDER DIFFERENCES AND FRIENDSHIP

Gender also shapes friendships. Women tend to have more friends. They report more intimacy with their friends, they have more emotionally expressive friendships, they make a greater commitment to the entire friendship, they disclose more personal information with their friends, and they are more likely to feel comfortable relying on their friends in times of stress.

Men are more likely to be intimate with women. They are likely to share their feelings and concerns with their partners than with male friends. Men also tend to have more instrumental friendships, they engage in activities (tennis, running, watching sports) with their friends, whereas women tend to talk to their friends about themselves, their lives, and their concerns (Wohlgemuth & Betz, 1991). In recent years, friendships between men and women have become more common. Such friendships can provide added social and emotional support for men and women. Social and cultural trends influence contemporary friendships.

Recent Social Changes Have Influenced the Nature of Contemporary Friendships:

+ Later marriage
+ Longer life expectancy
+ Egalitarian gender roles
+ Fewer children
+ Later life parenthood
+ Increased divorce rates
+ Greater mobility
+ Technology

The case of Pamela

Pamela has a successful career as an instructional designer. She has been offered and accepted increasingly higher status jobs in the past 20 years. Each new job required a move. Pamela is single and lives alone so she was able to move without too much difficulty. But each new city required developing a new set of friendships and relationships. Pamela maintained contact through Facebook and email with her old friends from other cities she has lived, but they are not around to do things with. Over the years, this system has worked well for Pamela, but now she is getting tired of always developing new relationships. Although she's extroverted and can meet people easily, Pamela is finding it difficult to continuously develop new friendships. She is considering retiring and moving back to Ohio to be near a sister and an old high school friend with whom she has kept in touch.

Relationships, be it friends or family, vary based on personal, social, and cultural factors. We may be closer to a particular family member or share our feelings more with some of our friends; the factors that make us like someone are complex.

WHAT MAKES US WANT TO BE FRIENDS WITH SOMEONE?

1. Physical attractiveness — matching hypothesis — people who are similar in terms of physical attractiveness prefer each other.
2. Similarity hypothesis — people who have similar race, religion, ethnicity, education, intelligence, and attitude are attracted to each other.
3. Reciprocity hypothesis — people tend to like and love those who like and love them.
    1. Compatibility
    2. Similar interests
    3. Mutual support
    4. Sharing
    5. Personal benefits

RELATIONSHIPS WITH SIBLINGS

This chapter has addressed the importance of relationships as a source of support in times of stress as a way of promoting health and happiness across adulthood. I have addressed relationships in a general way and not focused on intimate relationships. However I would like to close with one very important source of support in later life, especially for women — relationships with siblings. Our siblings are our longest relationships in our lives. In many cultures, this is the most primary relationship. Although there can be and are many conflicts with siblings, they provide each other with love and support throughout life. Studies have shown that sisters and brothers provide the most support and friendship for each other; it is one of our most important relationships across the lifespan, sisters in particular tend to be very close, especially in later life.

STRESSFUL RELATIONSHIPS

On a final chapter note, as well as providing support and aid during stressful times, relationships can and are a major source of stress. In the social sciences, relationships are generally viewed as having positive connotations. Relationships make us healthier and happier, and they provide us with support in times of stress and so forth. Relationships can of course also have a dark side. They can be stressful, destructive, hostile, and even dangerous. Relationships require hard work and sacrifice.

Research shows that most relationships are supportive and positive but sometimes are hostile or negative. They can cause more stress and have a negative impact on health, affecting blood pressure, contributing to heart disease, and other stress-related health concerns. It is important to evaluate your relationships to make certain that they are a source of satisfaction. Surround yourself with positive people whenever possible. Give and receive positive support in life, in order to be satisfied and happy in life, even to survive and make the world a better place, we need to have people in our lives. We also need to make a contribution to the well-being and happiness of others.

The word "paradise" comes from the Persian word that means garden. Many years ago, my Persian aunt told me to nurture my relationships as I would a tree or a plant in my garden. If you overwater or over-prune, it dies, if you do not attend to it, it dies; if on the other hand, you provide it with air, light, water, and appropriate trimming, in return, it will thrive and provide me and others with shade, fragrance, nurturance, and beauty.

REFERENCES

+ Abraham, I. L. (1991). The Geriatric Depression Scale and Hopelessness Index: Longitudinal psychometric data on frail nursing home residents. *Perceptual and Motor Skills, 72*, 875-880.

+ Adams, J.S. (1963). Towards an understanding of inequity. *The Journal of Abnormal and Social Psychology, 67*(5), 422-436.

+ Ainsworth, M.S. & Bowlby, J. (1991). An ethological approach to personality development. *American Psychologist, 46*(4), 333-341.

+ Alcoholism: Clinical & Experimental Research (2008, May 12). Men Are More Likely than Women to Crave Alcohol when They Feel Negative Emotions. Science Daily. Retrieved October 16, 2013, from http://www.sciencedaily.com /releases/2008/05/080511190834.htm

+ Alpert, E. (2013, August 27). More Americans are living alone, Census Bureau finds. *LA Times*. Retrieved October 3, 2013 from http://www.latimes.com/local/la-me-living-alone-20130828,0,5735939.story.

+ Anderson, G. (2010). Loneliness among older adults: a national survey of adults 45+. *AARP*. Retrieved August 15, 2013 from http://www.aarp.org/personal-growth/transitions/info-09-2010/loneliness_2010.html.

+ Antonucci, T.C., & Akiyama, H. (1991). Convoys of social support: Generational issues. In Pfeifer, Susan K., & Sussman M.B. (Eds.), *Marriage and Family Review, 16*(1,2), 103-124.

+ Antonucci, T. C. Akiyama, H. & Takahashi, K. (2004). Attachment and close relationships across the life span. *Attachment and Human Development, 6*, 353-370.

+ Baker-Miller, J. (1976). *Toward a new psychology of women*. Boston: Beacon Press. Bronfenbrenner, U. (1961). Some familial antecedents of responsibility and leadership. In L. Petrullo & B. M. Bass (Eds.), *Leadership and interpersonal behavior* (pp. 239-271). New York: Holt, Rinehart, & Winston.

+ Carstensen, L. L. (1992). Motivation for social contact across the life span: A theory of socio-emotional selectivity. In R. Dienstbier & J. E. Jacobs (Eds.)., *Nebraska symposium on motivation 1992: Developmental perspectives on motivation* (p.209-254). Lincoln: University of Nebraska Press.

+ Cattan, M., White, M., Bond, J., & Learmouth, A. (2005) Preventing social isolation and loneliness among older people: a systematic review of health promotion interventions. *Ageing & Society, 25*, 41-67.

+ Cecil, H., Stanley, M. A., Carrion, P. G., & Swann, A. (1995). Psychometric properties of the MSPSS and NOS in psychiatric outpatients. Journal of Clinical Psychology, 15(5), 593-602.

+ Cohen, S. (1988). Psychological models of the role of social support in the etiology of physical disease. *Health Psychology, 7*, 269-297.

+ Goldsher, H. (n.d.). Gender Differences in the Connection Between Social Support and Health. *Theravive*. Retrieved August 24, 2013 from http://www.theravive.com/research/ Gender-Differences-in-the-Connection-Between-Social-Support-and-Health.

+ Hobfoll, S. E., Freedy, J., Lane, C., & Geller, P. (1990). Conservation of social resources: Socialsupport theory. *Journal of Social and Personal Relationships, 7*, 465-478.

+ Holt-Lunstad, J., Smith, T.B, & Layton, J.B. (2010). Social relationships and mortality risk: A meta-analytical review. *PLOS Med 7*(7).

+ House, J. S., Landis, K. R., & Umberson, D. (1988). Social relationships and health. *Science, 241*, 540–545.

+ Kahn, R. L., & Antonucci, T. C. (1980). Convoys over the life course: Attachment, roles, and social support. In P. B. Baltes & O. G. Brim, Jr. (Eds.), *Life-span development and behavior* (Vol. 3, pp. 254-286). New York: Academic Press.

+ Kaplan, G.A., Seeman, T.E., Cohen, R.D., Knudsen, L.P., & Guralnik, J (1987).

+ Mortality among the elderly in the Alameda County Study: behavioral and demographic risk factors. *American Journal of Public Health, 77*(7), 818.

+ "Loneliness Research". (2013). *Campaign to End Loneliness*. Retrieved September 28, 2013 from http://www.campaigntoendloneliness.org/loneliness-research/

+ Major, B. N., Cozzarelli, C., Sciacchitano, A. M., Cooper, M. L., Testa, M., & Mueller, P. (1990). Perceived social support, self efficacy, and adjustment to abortion. *Journal of Personality and Social Psychology, 59*, 452-463.

+ Maslow, A. H. (1968). Toward a Psychology of Being. New York: D. Van Nostrand Company.

+ McShane, L. (2008, October 30). How to fight loneliness: 5 ways to happiness again! *Ezinearticles*. Retrieved September 13, 2013 from http://ezinearticles.com/?How-to-Fight-Loneliness---5-Ways-to-Happiness-Again!&id=2747889.

+ Obrist, P. A. (1981). *The cardiac-somatic relationship*. New York: Plenum Press.

+ Putnam, R.D. (2000). *Bowling Alone: The collapse and Revival of American Community*. New York: Simon & Schuster.

+ Taylor, S.E. (2002). *The tending instinct: How nurturing is essential to who we are and how we live*. New York: Holt

+ Welz, R., Veiel, H. O., & Hafner, H. (1988). Social support and suicidal behavior. In H. J. Moller, A. Schmidtke, & R. Welz (Eds.), *Current issues of suicidology* (pp. 322-327). Berlin: Spinger.

+ Wohlgemuth, E., & Betz, N. E. (1991). Gender as a moderator of the relationships of stress and social support in physical in college students. *Journal of Counseling Psychology, 38*(3), 367-374.

CHAPTER FIVE

Coping with Loss

CHAPTER FIVE

Coping with Loss

People are living longer than ever before. The average life expectancy has increased from about 49 years old in 1900 to about 80 years old in much of the developed world. Of course, everyone eventually dies. The increase in life expectancy, however, has influenced how we view death and dying. Throughout history, death has fascinated writers, poets, artists, and theologians. Technological advances have spared many of us active and premature engagement with death. However, if we live long enough, we will all lose someone we love.

Historically, death has been a daily companion for most people. People died in war, from childhood disease or in childbirth. Historically, infant mortality from infectious diseases was high. Most parents lost a child — one of the most painful losses in life. In the modern world, parents hope and plan to watch their children ripen into mature adults. Today most people expect to die late in life, usually from a chronic illness such as heart disease, cancer, or stroke — the three leading causes of death in America. Experiences with death are usually limited to the loss of an older relative such as a grandparent.

Even though most people do not contemplate their own death until later in life, death anxiety is still widespread and presents a threat to our health and well-being. Fear of losing someone we love also produces considerable stress. This chapter will explore contemporary notions of death, processes of bereavement, and the cultural and historical factors that influence the process of dying and view of death. Similar to other chapters in this book, there is much that is left unsaid; death, dying and bereavement are broad universal concepts that impact every human being on the face of the planet. This chapter presents some of the ways that we cope with death and dying in our contemporary society.

Regardless of when one is first forced to confront death, facing our own death or the death of a loved is difficult and stressful. The loss of a child, spouse or partner is of course the most difficult, but any loss is stressful and requires adjustment.

Most of us hope to avoid the loss of a child, but almost half the population will lose a partner. Most people hope to fall in love and get married. We meet someone, care for that person, and connect our life with them where day-to-day and long-term plans are interconnected. Then one day, sadly, we lose that person. Half of all people in a relationship will experience the loss of their partner. When that tragic event occurs, for a time, perhaps forever, life no longer has meaning. Any loss is stressful and requires significant adjustment; the loss of a partner involves the fundamental reconstruction of one's entire future.

Eventually and by necessity, the "survivor" must choose a new path that will determine the direction of his or her life. Without his or her partner, it will be a new and very different life. Sonia's case presented below illustrates just a few of the struggles that widows and widowers must face as they confront the loss of a beloved partner.

Sonia is a vibrant woman in her early 60s. She works as a nurse practitioner, has a large loving family. She has one grown child, many friends and she is happy and content with her life. The mainstay of her existence has been her husband of 28 years, Karl. In his early 70s Karl is an accountant who still works three days a week. While he struggled with health concerns in the past, including a heart condition, he has taken good care of himself. He hopes to live well into his retirement.

Whenever they can, Sonia and Karl bike and walk together. They both love to travel. They read the same novels and over a glass a wine discussed them late into the night. They have been making plans for retirement. They have been planning to sell their three-bedroom house, buy a smaller condo, and have more time and money for travel. They also have wanted to take a road trip and visit old college friends along the way.

Tragically and unexpectedly, Karl has another heart attack, one he did not survive. Karl's death thrust Sonia into a state of shock. As she slowly emerged from the intensity of her grief and her numbed state, she began to realize that she was facing a very new world. Her new reality was one in which all of her plans no longer appealed to her. She did not want to do the things that she and Karl had planned. Not only did she mourn and miss Karl, she also felt desperately sad that his life was shortened. She wasd also very confused and uncertain about her own future. Despite her son, her family, her friends, and her interests, her future looked bleak. She did not look forward to doing the things alone. She struggled to make sense of her new life. She had to find new meaning in her life as well as cope with the loss of her beloved husband.

In a sense the survivor must learn "to live again" and build a new life without his or her partner. The death of a loved one is one of the most tragic and stressful events a person experiences but is unfortunately an unavoidable aspect of life. Loss, grief, and mourning often lead to physical and psychological health concerns. Although every individual is unique in their reaction to the death of a loved one, there are factors that influence how bereavement and grief is experienced. How we cope with the loss of someone we care about is a very subjective and personal experience.

DEATH AND DEATH ANXIETY

How we think about death affects the process of bereavement. The intersecting influences of culture, age, personality, gender, religious beliefs, and social relationships shape how we view death and how we cope with the death of a loved one. Death has been worshipped, feared, and hated, but no one has really understood it. Studies show that fear of death creates significant anxiety for people of all ages and backgrounds.

For older men and women, anxiety about dying may be replaced with anxiety about dying "badly." Death anxiety results in an avoidance of death, a refusal to talk about death, and even a denial of death. Death anxiety appears to be greatest in mid-life, a time when one's accomplishments in life are questioned and one's sense of a limited time left to live becomes a concern. It is a time when we realize that we have lived the longest part of our life. Such a perception may compel us to worry about impending death, health, and accomplishment.

The loss of parents and loved ones compounds death anxiety. Studies indicate that women experience high levels of death anxiety, or at least they feel more comfortable expressing this anxiety. Indeed, women tend to be more comfortable expressing their distress and sadness. When distressed, for example, they are more comfortable crying. The expression of emotion and grief rituals vary by religion, but there are nonetheless commonalities in the expression of grief and loss. These include crying, anger, depression, sadness, numbness, and even immobility.

As people age, anxiety and concern over death shape worries about dying badly. Those who have religious faith and support tend to be less fearful of death. Those who have achieved their life goals are more ready to face the end of life and therefore demonstrate less fear of death. A person in great pain may wish for death — a release from pain and suffering.

What Is death?

Death is the end of existence, as we know it. It has a physical, a psychological, and a social component. Dying is a part of life, it is a life-long process — some people say that it begins at birth.

The limits of human existence are probably programmed into our genes; the best estimate of maximum human existence is approximately 120 years. Throughout history a small number of individuals have lived to be 100 years old. Social scientists are researching factors influencing longevity. They are studying people who live in "Blue Zones," areas around the world where people tend to live long and healthy lives (Tahmaseb-McConatha & Volkwein-Caplan, 2012). The lessons from such places are meaningful, but although life can be prolonged, ultimately we all die. Death is biological, psychological, and social.

1. Biological: cessation of the vital functions, when physical life ceases
2. Psychological: consciousness ceases to function, no thoughts, feelings, and needs; disappearance of personality characteristics
3. Social: end of institutional and cultural processes that surround a certain individual

FACTORS THAT INFLUENCE COPING WITH DEATH AND DYING

1. Death education: emphasizes anxiety reduction by achieving an increased understanding of death
2. Making plans for our own death (a final scenario)
3. Writing a will and a living will stating our wishes
4. Making funeral arrangements
5. Reminiscence about the past

Studies show that very few of us, only about 30% of US adults, prepare for their death. In all species, ensuring that life continues is a primary motivation. We can

trace much of our anxiety and fear of death to our wish to have life continue —
for ourselves, our offspring, our species, and our world. Social psychologists
have proposed theories that explain how we keep our fear of death at bay. Terror
management theory (Greenberg, Pyszczynski, & Solomon, 1986) is one attempt
to explain the pervasiveness of death anxiety.

According to this theory, which is based on the work of cultural anthropologist
Ernest Becker, people go through life feeling vulnerable — a vulnerability rooted
in the certainty that they will eventually die. As a result, they struggle to feel
good about themselves and find meaning in life. This theory is useful in helping
us understand why people engage in behavior that helps them to manage their
terror, anxiety, or fear of death. The theory explains how we manage our fears
and anxieties. Personal factors, such as self-esteem and personal resilience, can
buffer our fear of death. Other coping strategies, such as finding and focusing on
the meaning of life, making use of spiritual and religious beliefs, relying on social
and emotional support, can also be helpful. Values and beliefs in the afterlife and
reincarnation can mediate fear and anxiety over death.

HOW DO WE SHOW OUR ANXIETY ABOUT DEATH?

1. Avoiding situations that remind us of death, or not discussing issues related to death and dying.
2. Changing our lifestyle, developing healthy eating habits, exercising.
3. Dreaming, bargaining, and fantasizing about living a long healthy life.
4. Rejection of aging and staying away from older men and women.
5. Maintaining a stiff upper lip about the inevitable.

DEATH ACROSS THE AGES AND IN VARIOUS SOCIETIES

Most societies do not consider death to be the end of existence. Funerals and various death rituals are global occurrences. Death rituals have included songs, dances, different burial practices, mummification, and cremation ceremonies, all to prolong the existence of the deceased or to ensure entry into the next life. Belief systems and rituals influence how we understand and view death.

Death can be viewed as a way to eternal life, as a punishment for sins, as an end of everything, or as a normal part of existence. Views of death have changed throughout history and still vary around the world. In non-industrialized countries, experiences with death are still more common. In such societies, most people are still exposed to death in some way; it is more a part of daily life. The widespread experience of sickness, political unrest, terrorism, and natural disasters translate into an acute awareness of death — a sensitivity that may not exist in more industrialized stable societies such as the United States or Western Europe.

HISTORICAL VIEWS OF DEATH AND DYING

Although cultural differences in attitudes regarding death do exist, there are also some similarities. As people age their outlook about death gains a degree of similarity. There also appears to be a widespread belief in an afterlife, a belief that helps people to cope with the death of the loved ones. Even so, the inevitability of death has troubled us throughout ages. Archaeological and written evidence from the ancient Egyptians and early Greek philosophers indicate evidence of the fear of death. Ideas of the immortality of the soul were perhaps developed to reduce the fear of death. For example, ancient Egyptians left food and other necessities with their dead. American Indians buried their deceased with their possessions (Kubler-Ross, 1969). Both of these examples suggest a widespread belief in an afterlife in which worldly possessions may be needed.

Given the commonality of death during the Middle Ages, death was more accepted and perceived as a common misfortune (Jolley & Mitchell, 1996). During this time in Europe, it was generally believed the dead were sleeping until the Second Coming of Christ. There was also great concern when an individual succumbed to an untimely or sudden death because of the commonly held belief that individuals were judged at the moment of death. Therefore, if someone passed away suddenly, there was not sufficient time for confession or forgiveness. Deathbed confessions became important because people believed that they ensured that their soul would be taken by an angel and not the devil.

From the 18th century to the 19th century in Western Europe and in the United States living standards improved and people began to live longer lives. During this period death became a less common companion. Rather than being seen as an everyday natural occurrence, people considered it as sorrowful and remote. Death was viewed as an event that led to a happy reunion with deceased loved ones in paradise (Jolley & Mitchell, 1996).

With the onset technological innovation, the denial and avoidance of death gradually became a more common way to think about the end of life. People began to avoid the topic. Children were shielded from it; often even when it was obvious a person was dying, discussions of death were whispered or avoided.

CONTEMPORARY WAYS OF COPING WITH DEATH

In recent decades awareness of death and the process of dying has once again received research consideration. Attention has been paid to the process of dying and how people die. As discussed in Chapter 4, industrialization, geographic mobility, and a high divorce rate have changed the dynamics of social relationships and social support. As awareness and education on death and dying have become more prevalent, a variety of support systems have been developed to help the dying person and his or her family and friends. Such support includes the hospice movement, as well as support groups for those who are dying and for the bereaved. Such programs and groups help grieving family and friends cope with the death of a loved one.

Samuel lost his wife of 41 years to cancer. During the first few days after Helen's death, he was busy making arrangement and dealing with visitors. After everyone left he was grief-stricken for many weeks. Finally he began to realize that although he would always miss Helen, he was only 74 — he needed to continue living. Even so, he was unable to muster the energy to contact any of his friends or to continue with his hobbies of biking and writing. He realized he needed to talk about his new situation and get some support from people who were in a similar situation. He found a "Bereavement Group" at a local church and began attending meetings on Tuesday evenings. The members of the group talked about their losses. They reminisced about the past. They also talked about strategies for moving forward and making plans to enjoy as much of life as possible under new and changed circumstances.

After 7 weekly sessions, Samuel gradually began to feel that he was living again. He made some friends, both men and women. After the meetings, he began to have dinner with one or more of them. He returned calls to some of his and Helen's old friends and accepted invitations. He began to bike again. Slowly he started to feel a bit like his old self.

THE BENEFIT OF SUPPORT GROUPS

Support groups, especially specialized support assemblies such as bereavement groups can provide the important targeted support a person may be unable to get from their family or friends. Specialized support groups exist for alcohol problems, drug problems, cancer, weight loss, bereavement, and many other social, economic, cultural, physical, or psychological concerns. Support groups help the individual with the problem or concern. They also provide support for the friends and loved ones affected by the situation.

Bereavement support groups offer hope for the future, connections with others, a sense of universality, group cohesiveness, useful information, altruism, catharsis, self-understanding, help with existential questions, and social connection (Yalom, 1985). Participation in a bereavement group can help members benefit by being in contact with others who are struggling with similar issues. When a grieving person sees others heal, it provides a sense of encouragement like it did for Samuel.

We all face stressful life events such as the loss of a loved one. Some of us will choose to seek help from a support group while some people will not. Psychologists who have worked with grief have found that there tends to be three phases to the grief process. These stages vary significantly for each person.

1. **Initial Phase:** This begins with the death of someone and continues for weeks. Initial reactions include shock and disbelief. The grieving person may be numb, dazed, or disoriented. Symptoms may be physical and/or psychological.

2. **Intermediate Phase**: This phase begins several weeks after the death of a loved one and may last a year or longer. During this time, the bereaved must deal with the business associated with the life of the loved one. They may experience a variety of emotions including anger, guilt, loneliness, and longing. They may obsess about the lost love one and/or search for meaning in the loss.

3. **Recovery Phase**: Usually at least one year after a loss. The bereaved begins to look ahead and live their life again. They make plans, socialize, and move on with life. This does not mean that the loved one is forgotten or no longer missed. It means that the survivor has decided to live their life as fully as they can.

DEATH WITH DIGNITY

Modern death has become more remote, something that happens mostly late in life. Historically people died at home surrounded by family and loved ones. Contemporary deaths, by contrast, often occur in a sterile setting, such as a hospital, sometimes after the patient has been tortured with various painful "life-saving" medical procedures. On the one hand, modern medical advances prolong life and can help make dying less painful and more humane. On the other hand, medical procedures that prolong life can also lead to a painful and prolonged death. All too frequently, medical procedures continue long after there is a hope of recovery and the patient ends up being subjected to unnecessary suffering. New awareness about the importance of dying with dignity has prompted the training of practitioners who work with the dying. Professionals are receiving training so that they can respond with increased sensitivity to a dying person and his or her family.

There have been additional attempts to humanize the dying process. An increasing number of people are making end-of-life choices; they are refusing to die in hospitals, nursing homes, and asking to return to their homes in order to die in the company of loved ones. People prefer to die in the spaces and places in which they have spent their lives. They want to be surrounded by loved ones. Being able to exert a degree of control over their dying can help people cope with their fear of death. Recent programs have been designed to aid people in this process. One such program that does this is hospice.

WHAT IS HOSPICE?

Hospice is a historically based program designed to help people die with dignity. Throughout history travelers needed a place to rest, recuperate from illnesses, and die in peace. Hospice comes from the Latin word hospitium meaning "guest house." The contemporary philosophy and practice of helping people to die "a good death" is one that the hospice movement has emphasized. The modern notion of hospice was established in 1967 in London, England. St. Christopher Hospice and had several goals: 1) control and manage pain; 2) create an open,

intimate and supportive environment for the dying person and his or her family; and 3) maintain human dignity during the dying process. The first hospice opened in the United States in 1974. There are now more than 4,700 hospice programs in the United States ("What is hospice", n.d.).

Based on these principles, this multidisciplinary movement has grown in Europe and the United States. Each year, the movement helps more than one million people. The movement consists of ministers, priests, rabbis, nurses, doctors, social workers and others. Many of these men and women volunteer their time. The hospice movement can help with the dying process in someone's home, a hospital, a nursing home, or a hospice center. Most people who choose to utilize hospice wish to die as comfortably as possible in their own homes. The goal of hospice is to help provide a "good death." Palliative care is provided for the patient. The focus here is on the control of pain and symptoms, not treatment of illness or other procedures. The emphasis is to humanize the end of life experience and provide social support. Support is also provided for the family of the dying.

Hospice

1. Assist people at a very stressful time
2. Dying and mourning are a normal part of life; hospice gives its primary attention to the dying person, but they are also concerned with the family
3. Help patients die in a manner most comfortable for them and with dignity

The emphasis is on making the patient as comfortable as possible:
1. Control of pain
2. Enhance quality of life, so that both patient and family are able to deal with emotional issues
3. Provide an interdisciplinary team of caregivers that includes nurses, a medical director, volunteers, counselors, and social workers; this team emphasizes providing in-home care to the patient, and supportive load-reducing intervention for caregivers
4. Personal caring, contact, and discussion of death and dying between patients and medical staff
5. Do not overload patients with machines
6. Do not attempt to sweep death under the rug

Ellie's husband Thomas had advanced prostate cancer. Tom was no longer interested in continuing chemotherapy. He wanted to leave the hospital and go home to spend his last month as pain free as possible. He wanted to walk in his neighborhood and putter around in his garden. He wanted to spend time with Ellie and their children and grandchildren. The doctors told Thomas he had six months to one year to live if he stopped chemotherapy. Thomas and Ellie decided to make use of the local hospice service in their neighborhood.

Each day a nurse would visit Thomas, provide him his medications, check his symptoms and monitor his illness. Once a week Ellie took Thomas to see his doctor. A social worker and a priest both made regular visits. As Thomas's health deteriorated, the family was happy to have the support of the hospice team during this difficult period. Thomas died peacefully in his sleep 4 months after coming home. Ellie continued to receive the support of the hospice social worker for some weeks. She also joined a bereavement group at the local wellness center (a center which supports those who are ill, dying, and their families).

CULTURAL INDICATORS OF DEATH

As a way of coping with the loss of love ones and others, all societies have rituals and cultural indicators that acknowledge the life of the deceased and provide help for the bereaved. These rituals include special activities, particular gestures, special clothing, ceremonial objects, music, dance, singing, and any combination of the above that may help the bereaved cope with the loss of a loved one. Rituals have been performed throughout history. They include worship, rites of passage, celebrations, parades, and many other activities. Rituals associated with death are designed to remember and acknowledge the deceased and to help the grieving cope with their loss. They include:

1. Funerals
2. Specified periods of mourning
3. Lowered flags
4. Sympathy cards
5. Tombstones and cemeteries

The cultural indicators serve as coping resources that help survivors feel connected to others. They provide respect and remembrance for the departed. They help to acknowledge the deceased. They speak to the importance of the life of the deceased loved one and provide comfort and support for the bereaved.

Funerals and other rituals associated with death help the bereaved to acknowledge the reality of their loss. For centuries, philosophers and scholars have written about the impermanence of life. One of the first social science researchers in this area was Elizabeth Kubler-Ross (1981) who studied the reactions of those who were dying. In her research, Elizabeth Kubler-Ross interviewed hundreds of people who were dying. She found that when people found out they have a terminal illness, they tended to go through five stages:

1. **Denial**: This served as an important self-protective mechanism. It helps people keep from being overwhelmed; a means of protection; this is not limited to the dying person — family and friends also engage in denial.

2. **Anger**: Denial fades to partial acceptance along with anger; usually this anger is non-discriminating — directed at family, friends, God, anyone. It is generally a result of the belief of the unfairness of death. It is important for those who have contacts with people who are dying to be prepared for these bouts of anger.

3. **Bargaining**: Anger fades and is replaced with a desperate attempt to buy time. The dying person attempts to strike a bargain with God or anything to delay time of death; take medication, go to church, be kind, they may engage in magic or rituals.

4. **Depression**: As the fuller realization of impending death sets in, the person becomes depressed.

5. **Acceptance**: Eventually a quiet expectation and acceptance occurs. The patient may be weakened and tired. He or she may reminisce about life; it is a time of disengagement.

Kubler-Ross found that each stage was necessary and served an important function. There may be movement back and forth between denial and acceptance or the other stages. Some stages may occur simultaneously and not all people go through each. Contemporary social scientists take a life course approach to understanding death, dying, and bereavement: death influences your life choices throughout your lifespan.

Another psychologist who discussed end of life concerns was Eric Erikson (1950). The last two stages of Erikson's eight-stage model of human development relate to the topic of this chapter. In mid-life, adults focus on "generativity" or making a contribution to society. In the final stage of life called integrity versus despair, older men and women evaluate their life by focusing on their contributions. If they are happy and satisfied with what they have accomplished, they feel more prepared for the end of life.

The process of "life review" can help older men and women integrate their past experiences and come to terms with remaining inconsistencies. They can reach a place where they are comfortable with their past experiences. End of life research has found that as we approach the end we struggle to make sense out of our lives. By putting things in perspective, Erikson's theory provides a framework for this process.

For the dying person, there may also be personality changes that accompany the last days, months, or even years of life:

1. An increase in introspection and re-evaluation of life experiences occurs. This can take the form of reminiscence about the past, and they may even join a reminiscence group. This process is very therapeutic.
2. People can also engage in a life review process, which has positive aspects of reorganization and integration of the personality.
3. Disengagement from activities no longer satisfying or essential.

POSSIBLE OUTCOMES OF LATE LIFE REVIEW

As a result of the life review process proposed by Erikson, integrity tends to have positive consequences. It can lead to feeling good about one's self and one's life. This state of being tends to make one better prepared to face end-of-life issues. On the other hand, despair is another possible outcome of life review. Despair is characterized by regret and frustration; it can increase our fear of death.

BEREAVEMENT AND GRIEVING

It is important to grieve. Grieving helps with us cope with the death of a loved one. Grief is not a sign of weakness or self-indulgence. Rather it demonstrates a necessary and deep human need most of us have in response to the loss of a significant person in our lives. Failure to acknowledge our loss by grieving for our loved one can hinder the healing process. There is no "normal" time to grieve. Although places of employment often limit time for grieving by necessity, the process can continue for weeks, months, years, even a lifetime. Chronic grieving can continue for several years, and may include feelings of excessive guilt and self-blame.

Phases of Mourning:

Phase 1: The initial phase (the first few weeks) — shock, and disbelief, numbness, anxiety attacks, depression, an obsession with the deceased.

Phase 2: The intermediate phase (generally up to one year, longer in some cultures) — the survivor attempts to find meaning in life, resume some activities, return to work.

Phase 3: Recovery phase (one year to the remainder of the survivor's life) — the decision is made to become a survivor, develop reconstructed plans and goals.

Grief is an overwhelming emotion of loss. It can come from the loss of a loved one or from learning that one is terminally ill. It is associated with numbness, a removal from pleasurable activities, and perhaps immobilization. Grief is a universal experience although everyone experiences it differently. Cultural expectations often shape the rules associated with how grief is expressed.

Grief is accompanied by mourning and bereavement. Although grief is most commonly associated with death, any element of loss can bring about some form of grief. The impact of a loss is determined by the meaning or value an individual assigns to the loss. Grief should not be ignored. Psychologists have found that the denial of grief can become dangerous to the person's long-term health and happiness. Every life change, no matter how small, contains some element of change and therefore some amount of loss. Grief associated with death, especially death of someone close, such as a spouse or a child, is the most severe, intense, and painful form of the experience. The tragic death of a spouse or child can disrupt one's whole life and thrust our emotions into the canyons of despair and anguish.

Grief, then, is often acute, immobilizing and long-lasting. It is one of life's most devastating emotions — one that at least half of us will face. Yet, most of us are ill prepared to cope with our grief and bereaved feelings.

BEREAVEMENT

Bereavement is a universal part of love and loss. It is also an important coping strategy. Bereavement practices have wide variability. For example, certain European mourning codes arose in the early 19th century. The codes established proper mourning attire and proper funeral rites, an integral part of the bereavement ritual. Poor families would save enough money so that they could provide their deceased love one a proper funeral. In the 20th century many of the culturally delegated mourning practices, such as mourning dresses, disappeared. The bereavement attitudes and practices of Puritan New England, which focused on simplicity, had an impact on culture in the United States. Funeral rituals became less elaborate and public mourning practices diminished. The Puritan attitude forbade outward signs of grief and excessive mourning. There are also ethnic differences in the funeral and bereavement practices in the US. Bereavement and the practices accompanying bereavement vary; however, regardless of the practice, bereavement is an important process in a person's attempt to adjust to the loss of a loved one.

Death is a part of the human experience. In most contemporary societies, educational courses, literature, and the media have begun to address death realistically. These outlets have focused on how to help the grieving person cope with the loss of a loved one. Although these important steps have improved our attitudes toward death, it is human nature to fear the unknown. Death is still a fearful, frightening event. Fear of death is still widespread, even universal. Such deeply rooted sentiments are not likely to disappear in the near future. What has changed, though, is our way of coping and dealing with death.

COPING WITH LOSS

Everyone copes differently. There are a number of ways of coping with loss. This book has focused on social and physical activity as ways of coping with stress. The loss of a loved one is no exception. Social activity, social engagement, and social involvement all help us heal. Social support has been identified as a primary factor that may alleviate the negative effects of the death of a loved one and aid the bereavement process.

Social support serves as an intervening variable that mediates stressful life events. It is a buffer against negative life events and helps to reduce the negative effects of stress on both physical and psychological well-being. Social support contributes to positive development and personal well-being and provides an individual with the "psychological supplies" that contribute to the maintenance of mental and emotional well-being. Consistent findings conclude that among various populations, psychological distress increases when there is a lack of social support (Tahmaseb-McConatha & Volkweing-Caplan, 2012).

CONTROL AS A COPING MECHANISM

Although everyone dies, feeling a degree of control over one's life is one way of coping with loss. As discussed earlier, some control can be exerted over where and how one dies. For the bereaved, losing someone can lead to feelings of helplessness and a loss of control over one's life While everything can never be controlled, regaining a measure of control can be healing and therapeutic (Tahmaseb-McConatha, McConatha, Deaner, & Dermigny, 1995; Tahmaseb-McConatha & Volkweing-Caplan, 2012; Schultz and Heckhausen, 1996). Researchers have proposed that one of the most important factors that determines an individual's reaction to life experiences is his or her perception of control. Feelings of being "in control" are inversely related to feelings of powerlessness, depression, and social isolation. Feelings of being "out of control" are conversely associated with negative psychological and physiological responses. Psychologists have worked on helping people gain control over their lives. When we feel out of control, we exhibit behavioral, motivational, cognitive, and emotional deficits (Seligman, 1989).

The feeling that no one is able to understand the feelings and hardship of a bereaved individual is commonplace. If someone has not shared the same experience/loss, the bereaved individual may not be able to find comfort in their support, friendship, caring, concern, or kind words. Tedeschi and Calhoun (1993) note that the isolation of bereavement occurs because the bereaved individual holds the perception that others who have not experienced the same loss/situation cannot possibly understand them. Staying active and engaged

and connecting with others who share the experience of loss can be helpful in coping. Benjamin, a 75 year-old widower who was retired, lost his wife of 48 years after a painful battle with cancer. He was close to his two adult children and three grandchildren. He was also very active. He liked to walk, volunteer, and go to church. His views were generally positive although he missed his wife desperately. Much of his attitude derived from the fact that his wife had suffered and was looking forward to her release from pain. Both Benjamin and his wife were also religious, and Benjamin believed that his wife had gone to "a better place." Benjamin adjusted to the loss of his wife by staying active, praying, and relying on his networks of support. Despite the fact that he missed her and always would, he continued to enjoy aspects of his life. In short, he found himself loving life as fully as he could.

Susanna presents another example of someone struggling with loss.

Suzanna was 64-year-old manager at an employment agency. She had a good job and was well educated. One and half years ago, she lost her husband of 18 years to a heart attack. She had a good relationship with her brother and stepchildren and an extended network of close friends. Although it was difficult for Susanna to move on with her life after losing her husband, she stayed in close contact with family and friends and stayed socially engaged. She enjoyed holidays, Sunday dinners, talking on the phone, reading, watching movies, walking, gardening, photography, going out for breakfast and/or dinner, and talking with friends. At first, she forced herself to stay busy with these activities. After a time, she realized that she once again enjoyed them and was grateful to have stayed active and engaged. It is now not difficult for any of these normally enjoyable activities to make her very happy.

THE IMPORTANCE OF PHYSICAL ACTIVITY

Throughout this book, I have focused on the importance of physical activity as a way of coping with stress. Stress associated with the death of a loved one is no exception. Any form of exercise can help one feel better. It certainly does not make the pain go away, but it can boost the body and provide much needed relief. Exercise

increases overall health and well-being. Regular exercise reduces symptoms associated with depression and anxiety. Exercise also can also help with sleep, which is often disrupted by stress. Exercise also promotes a feeling of control and can lead to social engagement, two coping strategies discussed. There are many websites that provide support and information on how to cope with loss. Below are tips from the following American Cancer Society site ("Coping with loss", 2013):

1. Allow yourself to experience your feelings. Don't tell yourself how to feel or let others tell you how you should feel.
2. Be patient with yourself and the process. Don't pressure yourself with expectations. Remember each person is different and heals in his or her own way and time. No one knows how you should heal.
3. Get support. Talk about your loss, your memories, and your experience of the life and death of your loved one.
4. Try to maintain your normal lifestyle. Do not make any major changes for a while.
5. Stay or become active. Take care of yourself. Eat well and exercise. Physical activity is a good way to release tension.

6. Avoid an unhealthy lifestyle. Avoid drinking too much alcohol or using other drugs.

7. Forgive yourself for all the things you did or didn't say or do. Compassion and forgiveness for yourself and others is important in healing.

8. Do not focus on your grief all the time. Find distractions.

9. Prepare for holidays, birthdays, and anniversaries knowing that strong feelings may come back. Decide how you want to celebrate.

10. Write a letter to the person who died to say everything you wish you could say to them. Make a scrapbook.

REFERENCES

+ "Coping with loss". (2013, February 4) *American Cancer Society*. Retrieved September 28, 2013 from http://www.cancer.org/treatment/treatmentsandsideeffects/emotionalsideeffects/griefandloss/coping-with-the-loss-of-a-loved-one-coping-with-loss

+ Erikson, E. (1950). *Childhood and society*. New York, NY: Norton

+ Greenberg, J., Pyszczynski, T., & Solomon, S. (1986). The causes and consequences of a need for self-esteem: A terror management theory. *Public Self and Private Self*. New York, NY: Springer.

+ Jolley, J. M., & Mitchell, M. L. (1996). *Lifespan Development: A Topical Approach*. Madison, WI: Brown and Benchmark.

+ Kubler-Ross, E. (1969). *On death and dying*. New York, NY: Macmillian.

+ Kubler-Ross, E. (1981). *Living with death and dying*. New York, NY: Macmillian.

+ Schulz, R., & Heckhausen, J. (1996). A life span model of successful aging. *American Psychologist, 51*(7), 702-714.

+ Seligman, M. E. P. (1989). Research in clinical psychology: Why is there so much depression today? In I. Cohen (Ed.), *The G. Stanley Hall Lecture Series, Vol. 9*, Washington, DC: American Psychological Association.

+ Tahmaseb McConatha, J., McConatha, D., Deaner, S., & Dermigny, R. (1995). A computer based intervention for the education and therapy of institutionalized older adults. *Educational Gerontology, 21*, 141-150.

+ Tahmaseb-McConatha, J. & Volkwein-Caplan, K. (2012). *The Social Geography of Aging*. Oxford, England: Meyer & Meyer.

+ Tedeschi, R. G., & Calhoun, L. G. (1993). Using the support group to respond to the isolation of bereavement. *Journal of Mental Health Counseling, 15*(1), 47-54.

+ "What is hospice". (n.d.). *Hospice Foundation of America*. Retrieved September 28, 2013 from http://www.hospicefoundation.org/whatishospice.

+ Yalom, I. D. (1985). *The theory and practice of group psychotherapy*. USA: Basic Books.

CHAPTER SIX

Laugh and Pray

with Malathi Dissanayake

CHAPTER SIX

Laugh and Pray

with Malathi Dissanayake

Sara and Alison are planning a vacation. For five years, they have looked forward to a trip to Europe. The trip is now six months away. Alison is excited about planning their days. She loves to travel. When she returns from a trip, she feels a sense of happiness and contentment with her life. However, making travel arrangements causes overwhelming anxiety. Every time, she considers the necessary arrangements, Sara becomes nervous and feels overwhelmed. What if she makes a mistake? What if the hotels she chooses are awful? Sara wants to consult a travel agent. Alison, her frequent traveling companion, will not hear of it. She lacks Sara's anxiety about planning the trip. She is not concerned about choosing hotels, cities, or trains. She asks Sara to let her make all the travel plans. Alison loves making arrangements, and she has no problem if things do not work out as she hoped. For her it is part of the pleasure and adventure of traveling. Such a decision brings her a sense of satisfaction and frees Sara of the anxiety and stress of planning and arrangement.

As the case of Alison and Sara illustrates, even pleasurable events can prove to be stressful. What is considered stressful depends on a complicate mix of personality, resources, culture, and even what is going on in the moment. As earlier chapters of this book have illustrated, understandings of stress are complex. Everyone perceives and manages stress differently. There are, however, several ways of coping with stress that have proven to be effective regardless of the individual or culture. These include humor and laughter, relying on spirituality or religion, and of course focusing on factors that increase life satisfaction and happiness. In this chapter, I explore these proven coping methods. There are, of course, many other effective ways of coping with stress, some of which have been addressed in previous chapters and many of which are beyond the scope of one book on stress.

THE HEALING POWER OF LAUGHTER

Humor has been known to promote positive mental health. Laughter clearly has therapeutic properties. Everyone knows that they feel better when they laugh. Research has supported the therapeutic value of humor as a coping mechanism, a source of tension relief, and even as a mechanism of survival.

Humor also has a positive physiological impact. During psychotherapy, clinicians often rely upon humor. For example, in one early study, working with depressed patients, Nussbaum and Michaux (1963) found that humor positively correlated with improved clinical ratings. A number of other studies have subsequently explored the use of humor as a therapeutic tool and found support for the use of humor in therapy. If humor is used positively and productively, it can help ease tension and anxiety.

Humor transcends all ages, cultures, and personality styles. It therefore is a potentially useful tool for coping with a wide variety of stressful events. It can be used to defuse a stressful situation, which in turn lessens the potentially negative impact of stress.

The Benefits of Humor

1. **Physiological**: leads to a release of tension in the body.
2. **Psychological**: results in a pleasurable experience, a tension release, a new perspective.
3. **Educational**: humor can lead to insight, a new perspective on a stress-related problem.
4. **Social**: humor can connect us with others, lead to a sense of social inclusion, bonding.

Humor has many benefits associated with managing stress. It can help us manage our emotions; it can be useful when coping with change and uncertainty, it can provide perspective. It is surprising that humor is not utilized more frequently as a coping mechanism. Years ago, Norman Cousins cured himself of a potentially fatal disease by ingesting high doses of vitamins and watching funny television programs and movies. Cousins believed that humor helped cure him (Cousins, 1981). His book resulted in a renewed interest in the healing powers of humor.

As Cousins' case demonstrates, humor can help people recover from illnesses, cope with stress, and confront death anxiety. It also enhances the immune system and reduces feelings of pain (Compton & Hoffman, 2013). Utilizing humor in later life has numerous benefits, including the promotion of higher self-esteem, decreasing the incidence of depression, reducing anxiety, and advancing a more positive self-concept.

NEGATIVE HUMOR

Not all humor, though, is therapeutic or beneficial. Ageist humor, which depicts older men and women in a variety of disrespectful ways, can have a negative impact on the self-image, health, and well-being of older men and women. Negative images of "old age" are widespread in birthday cards, television programs, films, books, and magazines. Many studies have shown that the media shapes social meanings. Media images have considerable influence on the development of beliefs, values, and attitudes toward age, aging, and ageism.

The cultivation hypothesis suggests that in technologically advanced societies, such as the United States and Germany, people often rely on the mass media as a primary source of cultural information and socialization. If older men and women are depicted as forgetful, depressed, unattractive, ill, disabled or even ready to die, younger adults and children internalize these images. Indeed, advertising is a powerful tool through which people construct their sense of culturally appropriate attitudes and beliefs. Humorous ageist messages promote the belief that it acceptable to denigrate older men and women as long one is doing it humorously. The widespread of use of negative and ageist humor can lead to an increase in stress, anxiety, and depression in older men and women (Palmore, 2004).

The positive psychology movement has increased public attention regarding the potential constructive benefits of humor as a coping mechanism (Seligman &

Csikszentmihalyi, 2000). Studies have found that humor can improve outlook and increase happiness and life satisfaction (Labouvie-Vief & Medler, 2002). Humor is also useful in coping with anxiety and depression associated with bereavement (Hill, 2005). As much as possible, it is therapeutic to laugh at life's ups and downs. Humor and laughter can reduce overall stress and promote a more positive view of ourselves. Humor can serve as a natural stress-reducer that leads to improved health, increased life expectancy, and overall well-being.

Developing a sense of humor can be a useful coping strategy for dealing with life stress. Elizabeth Scott (2013) provides the following guidelines for increasing our capacity for humor and utilizing humor as a coping strategy.

1. **Start with a Smile**
   Studies show that having a smile on your face can release endorphins, which make you feel better.
2. **Take a Step Back**
   When you're in the middle of a difficult situation, it can seem overwhelming. If you try to see your situation as an observer would, it's often easier to recognize what's funny. Work on reframing your perspective.
3. **Value the Extremes**
   If your situation seems ridiculously frustrating, recognize the potential humor in just how ridiculously frustrating and annoying it is. In your imagination, take the situation to an extreme that becomes even more ridiculous until you find yourself amused.
4. **Have a Funny Buddy**
   Find a friend with whom you can laugh, and let the relationship work for you!
5. **Make It a Game**
   You can have a "most annoying boss" contest with your friends.
6. **Watch Funny Shows and Movies**
7. **Read Funny Books**
8. **Visit Funny Websites**
9. **Join Funny Clubs**
10. **Getting your Friends on Board with Laughter**

Developing a sense of humor in dealing with stressors in life is free and therapeutic. Humor as a way of coping can help us deal with difficulty situations, it can make others around us feel better, and it can even help us be physically healthier and psychologically happier.

SPIRITUALITY AND COPING

Spirituality provides meaning and purpose in life. It leads to a feeling of connectedness with others and with nature and art (Starks & Hughey, 2003; Berk, 2007). According to psychologist Viktor Frankl, a Holocaust survivor who chronicled his experiences in a concentration camp, it is important to find meaning in all of life's situations, regardless of how difficult. Frankl addressed spirituality, freedom, and responsibility as three important and distinct human qualities (Santrock, 2004). Spirituality has a unique meaning for each person and, although it is often associated with religion, it does not necessarily have a religious basis.

Spirituality associated with organized religion is on the decline in the West. Contemporary forms of spirituality are often related to Eastern philosophical traditions such as Buddhism. People need spiritual nourishment. However, secularism is on the rise in Western societies.

For example, a recent Pew Research Center found that more than a fifth of Jewish Americans say they have no religion although they identify themselves as culturally Jewish. Less than a third of Jews — even religious Jews — think someone can't be Jewish without believing in God. It seems that more Americans of all faiths are turning away from organized religions (Alpert, 2013).

Many people prefer to focus their spiritual energies in directions not associated with organized religion. Nevertheless spirituality is an important component of many people's lives. A well-known study, the MacArthur study of adult development, found spirituality to be an important aspect of many people's lives (Brim, 1999). As the case of William Miller illustrates, spirituality and/or religiosity is related to positive life goals, integrity, and life satisfaction.

The case of William Miller presented earlier provides an affirming example of the healing power of spirituality and religion. William Miller grew up as an angry, abused young man. By the time he was in his 20s, he had been in and out of jail for fighting, drinking, and disorderly conduct. In his mid-20s, he met and fell in love with lovely young women, Sara. Sara was deeply religious; both the spiritual aspects and the community of support she enjoyed from the other members of the church were very important to her. William had never considered religion to be important. In order to please Sara, he began to attend church. Surprisingly he found himself truly believing the messages he heard each Sunday from the kind and charismatic minister of Sara's church. For almost one year, he would accompany Sara to church every week. After this time he truly believed the messages of Sara's Christian church; he felt he was calmer, happier, less angry, and ready to "make something of himself" as he puts it and help others.

Mr. Miller is now in his 80s and although his life has been hard, he is still married to Sara, they have raised more than 20 children, 6 of their own and 14 children who needed a home. They took homeless, parentless children in and raised them, providing them with a home and lots of love. William's 80-plus years have been filled with hardship, but he is still a very spiritual and positive person. Miller's strength comes from his faith, his church, Sara, and his family. As an African-American, he also experienced years of racial discrimination and prejudice, but he says that his faith helped him forgive and forget.

Spirituality generally increases with age (Wink & Dillon, 2002). Women appear to find spirituality and religiosity to be more important in their lives, especially in later life (Cowlishaw, Niele, Teshuva, Browning, & Kendig, 2013). Spirituality and religiosity can lead to increased meaning in life (Berk, 2007). Spirituality often takes the form of organized religion, although this is not an essential component of spirituality. However for many people the social and community support derived from an organized religion can promote well-being and support in coping with stressful life events.

Religion has played an important part in the development of most cultures. Many wars have been fought for a religious purpose. Religion guides people and helps them adjust to stressful life circumstances. Some religious coping acts

are prayer, seeking support, and getting strength from God and other members of the religion. Older adults use religion as a way to cope with stressful events that can erode their self-esteem and feelings of self-worth. Studies have shown that spirituality (religious activity) is an important coping mechanism for people suffering from the chronic conditions often associated with later life. Studies have indicated that people who are religious fear their own death and that of their loved ones less.

RELIGION AND SPIRITUALITY

Spirituality and religion are different concepts (Berk, 2007). Religion has been defined as a doctrine of beliefs that is formally organized and helps individuals find meaning in life. It is also considered a support system and an important part of healing. Religion tends to be based on an organized religious belief system and is often connected to physical spaces and rituals.

Throughout the history of world, people have found meaning in organized and non-organized religions. One study found that 98% of participants in India, 88% in Italy, and 72% in France state that they believe in God (Gallup, 1987). Religious identity seems to be one of the strongest factors that influence one's self-concept (Guttmann, 2003). A study with Sri Lankans revealed that religious identification is the most important component of Sinhalese self-identities (Dissanayake & McConatha, 2011). Study after study indicates that people's religious orientation is associated with psychological well-being (Maltby & Day, 2003).

Religious orientations can be:

1. Intrinsic orientation toward religion: People who fall into this category are fully committed to their religious beliefs. Also, religion has a significant impact on all aspects of their lives (Allport, 1966). Intrinsic orientation toward religion seems to be related to a sense of competence and control, freedom from worry and guilt, and an absence of illness (Ventis, 1995).

2. Extrinsic orientation toward religion: People who fall in this category tend to consider religion as an opportunity for participation in an in-group (Genia & Shaw, 1991), as well as religious involvement (Fleck, 1981). They also think that it will provide social status, protection, social support (Allport & Ross, 1967), and is an ego-defense (Kahoe & Meadow, 1981).

3. A quest orientation toward religion (Baerveldt, Bunkers, DeWinter, & Kooistra, 1998; Beit-Hallahmi & Argyle, 1997; Gorsuch, 1988; Wulff, 1997): These tend to be people who are open to religious experiences but are still searching. Many of the new converts to the Buddhist tradition fall into this category.

Interest in religion, especially organized relation, appears to be related to age (Santrock, 2004). As people, age religion plays a more important role there. Older Americans, for example, become more religious or spiritual with age (Wink & Dillon, 2002). They are also more likely to participate in religious activities as well as watch religious TV programs (Princeton Religion Research Center, 1999).

Although surveys indicate that Europeans tend to be less "religious" than Americans, similar outcomes have been found cross-culturally. For example, similar to Americans, religiosity grows stronger in older Canadians (Jones, 2003).

Spirituality and faith changes and develops throughout across the lifespan. Theorists have proposed stages of faith development. For example, James Fowler (1981) has described five stages in the development of faith that range from childhood to late adulthood (Berk, 2007). According to Fowler, older adults become more conscious about their own belief system and tend to consider the importance of religious symbols and rituals. Further, they become more open to other religious views as sources of motivation (McFadden, 1996).

Men and women also tend to experience spirituality differently. For example, women seem to have a strong interest in religion compared to men. Women tend to feel that religion is a key dimension of their lives, attend organized and personal religious activities, and believe in God or his presence more than men. Compared to men, women are more likely to join a religious congregation, become involved in religious practices, and report that they seek connectedness with God (Wink & Dillon, 2002).

Gender differences in spirituality may be related to stressful aspects of women's lives. For example, women feel more stress and anxiety due to poverty, widowhood and caregiving (Berk, 2007). Older women are more likely than men to experience the pain of loss through widowhood. Such a loss, discussed in earlier chapters can lead to psychological and social problems such as stress, depression, and social isolation. Providing care for the chronically ill family members may add more stress, particularly for women. The stress that arises from these problems may cause them to rely more on religion for emotional and social support to cope with stress (Berk, 2007).

There are also ethnic group differences in relation to elders' religious involvement. For example, elders from various ethnic minorities in the United States, African-American, Native American, and Hispanic, tend to be more engaged in both organized and informal religious activities. Churches play an important community support role for many minority elders. Studies have shown that many African American and Hispanic elders may lack resources or they may mistrust psychologists and therapists and therefore rely on their churches and religious beliefs during difficult times. Institutions of religion provide education, health service, social welfare, and political involvement to improve the quality of life (Berk, 2007).

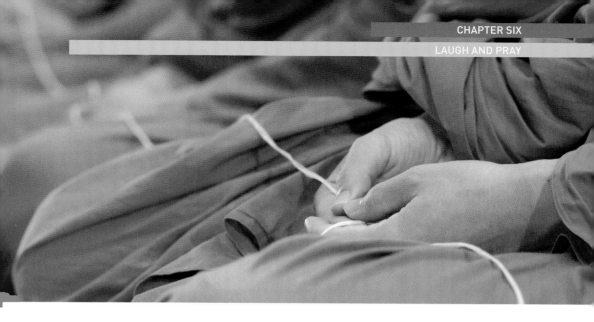

Religion tends to provide an important source of support and resources for African-American elders (Armstrong & Crowther, 2002). Compared to Caucasians, a greater number of African-American elders say that they work with God to find solutions during stressful times (Krause, 2005). Studies have found that the belief in God's powers in minority older adults plays a part in their optimism, self-esteem, and life satisfaction (Krause, 2005; Schieman, Pudrovska, & Milkie, 2005).

Clearly a sense of spirituality and a connection to a religion can prove to be major sources of support and play an important role in reducing stress for older adults. Attending church mass provides them an opportunity to collaborate with God, to share their feelings and thoughts with members of the same age and to meet with friends and religious group leaders. It can help reduce loneliness and isolation, strengthen social connections, and provide emotional satisfaction, and even reduce fear of death.

BENEFITS OF RELIGIOUS INVOLVEMENT AND SPIRITUALITY

Studies have found a positive relationship between religious participation and longevity (Thoresen & Harris, 2002). A longitudinal study has revealed that organized, as well as informal, religious involvement helps individuals have long life (Helm, Hays, Flint, Koenig, & Blazer, 2000; Strawbridge, Shema, Cohen, &

Kaplan, 2001). As previously mentioned, religious involvement helps individuals deal with negative life events and stressors in their lives, and positive religious coping helps reduce the symptoms of psychological distress.

Religious beliefs can help reduce stress (Santrock, 2004). They can motivate people to feel better about themselves and become more determined and courageous, especially during difficult times. Religious thoughts and beliefs help maintain hope. People may be more likely to hope for the best and persevere with goals and plans amid crisis if they have strong religious beliefs or believe in higher power.

Religion also helps prevent psychological problems, such as depression and anxiety (Santrock, 2004). People who participate in religious activities have the opportunity to share their feelings and thoughts with others and thereby experience greater relief. Religious places and religious groups seem to be accessible and inexpensive sources of emotional and social support especially for older men and women. The availability of support systems provided by organized relations can prevent loneliness and isolation, a significant problem among older adults.

Religion seems have a positive impact on individuals' overall well-being. Religion and religious involvement often guide people to engage in behaviors that promote healthy living. Some religious beliefs also prohibit alcohol and tobacco use thereby promoting health awareness and a healthier lifestyle. As a result, those who are religious tend have lower drug and alcohol use than non-religious people (Gartner, Larson, & Allen, 1991). Religious beliefs help people engage in health-promoting behaviors that affect their overall well-being.

Organized religious institutions provide the opportunity to develop social relationships. Earlier in this book, I presented information on the multiple benefits of positive relationships. Such relationships lead to increased happiness and well-being (Kang, Shaver, Sue, Min, & Jing, 2003).

Relationships provide emotional satisfaction. Emotional satisfaction is important for individuals to maintain physical well-being and to have fewer health issues. Experiencing positive emotions in daily life seems to be an important factor in building psychological, social, and physical resources that promote overall well-being (Fredrickson, 2001).

People's emotional states are associated with both physical and psychological health (Hu & Gruber, 2008). That is, both positive and negative effects are related to the determinants of health functioning, such as distress, daily functioning, and quality of life among older adults with chronic illnesses. Hence, religious activities, religious groups and gatherings may provide an opportunity for individuals to connect with others (Collins, Dunke-Schetter, Lobel, & Scrimshaw, 1993), thereby gaining emotional satisfaction in later life.

Later life is a time filled with challenges, but it can also be a time of deep meaning and connection. Spirituality and religiosity can be helpful with these important aspects of well-being. They can also help answer important life review questions such as: What does it all mean? What happens next? Spirituality and religiosity are important elements of later life leading to satisfaction and fulfillment. Even if organized religion has not played a significant role in the lives of younger adults, as people age they often seek comfort and support in an organized religion.

Diane and John both come from a Christian background. They have been married for 26 years, and during that time the only time they have gone to a church was when they were visiting family or for a wedding or funeral. They have no children so they never considered a religious upbringing or education for their offspring. They have recently both retired and are healthy, active, and happy. However, suddenly they both feel a desire for a more organized spiritual connection. They decide to visit a different church each month in the hopes that they might find one that appear to them. Eventually they settle on a local Unitarian Church that allows them the freedom to believe what they wish and yet provides them with the ritual and spiritual connection they were both looking for. They also make new friends in the church, which enriches their lives further.

The case of Diane and John is not an unusual situation for contemporary older men and women. Studies show that secularism is on the rise. Many people fulfill their spiritual needs through support groups, yoga, Buddhist teachings, or simply by quietly following the beliefs with which they were raised. Travelling throughout Europe one notices that on Sundays the churches are relatively empty, yet if one asks people, especially older people, they tend to say that their belief systems are strong and provide them with support during difficult times.

Diane and John chose to join a church; others may turn to rituals provided by philosophical traditions, such as Buddhism. Lewes Richmond (2011) in a *Huffington Post* article provides the following guidelines for spiritual practice. These guidelines are derived from Buddhist philosophical views. The Buddhist tradition offers spiritual practices for cultivating happiness.

Gratitude. When people are asked what they like about being older, they often answer „gratitude,“ gratitude for children, grandchildren, good health, free time, wearing what they want, the chance to travel, giving back to the community.

Generosity. It is free and promotes happiness and well-being. One happiness study reported that if giving weren't free, drug companies could market a great new drug called „give back“ instead of Prozac.

Reframing. Aging includes its share of reverses, losses and sorrows. What makes the difference is our attitude about them. If a bad knee means we can't jog anymore, we needn't despair; we can take up swimming. We tend to think of time as linear and horizontal, but it is also vertical — one breath at a time. Vertical time is really breath-based reframing.

Curiosity. Curiosity is an important attitude to cultivate as we age. Physical exercise grows new muscle, mental activity grows new brain cells, and emotional engagement lifts the spirit. Curiosity keeps us young; we need to cherish it. If you see an interesting ad for a wildlife class, consider taking it.

Flexibility. Things change as we age, and some of those changes are irrevocable. Our youthful stamina is gone forever; a dying friend will never return. In the face of these changes, it's important that we not become rigid. With every reversal comes new opportunity. Research shows that people with an active involvement in church or spiritual community live on average seven years longer than those who don't.

There is no clear answer to the questions of religion and spirituality and its impact on stress and health. Like many other aspects of life, the relationship between religion, spirituality, and well-being is complicated. Clearly some of the most religious places in the world are very stressful places. In this chapter, I reviewed some of the ways that both religion and spirituality, not necessarily the same thing, can increase well-being and promote happiness.

REFERENCES

+ Allport, G. W. (1966). The religious context of prejudice. *Journal for the Scientific Study of Religion, 5*, 447-457.

+ Allport, G. W. & Ross, J. M. (1967). Personal religious orientations and prejudice. *Journal of Personality and Social Psychology, 5*, 432-433.

+ Alpert, E., (2013). "Jewish secularism on the rise, pew study finds". *Los Angeles Times*. Retrieved October 4, 2013 from http://articles.latimes.com/2013/sep/30/local/la-me-1001-jewish-not-religious-20131001

+ American Association of Retired Persons. (1995). Mature Americans in the 90s. [Brochure]. Roper Organization.

+ Armstrong, T. D., & Crowther, M. R. (2002). Spirituality among older African-Americans. *Journal of Adult Development, 9*, 3-12.

+ Baerveldt, C., Bunkers, H., DeWinter, M., & Kooistra, J. (1998). Assessing a moral panic relating to crime and drugs policy in the Netherlands: towards a testable theory. *Crime Law and Social Change, 29*, 31–47.

+ Beit-Hallahmi, B., & Argyle,M. (1997). *The psychology of religious behaviour, belief and experience*. London: Routledge.

+ Berk, L. E. (2007). *Development through the lifespan* (4th Ed.). Boston, MA: Allyn & Bacon.

+ Berman, D. (1998). Late-blooming scholars. *Business Week*, 3587, 106.

+ Brim, O. (1999). *The MacArthur Foundation study of midlife development*. Vero Beach, FL: MacArthur Foundation.

+ Chafetz, P. K., Holmes, H., Lande, K., Childress, E., & Glazer, H. R. (1998). Older adults and the news media: Utilization, opinions, and preferred reference term. *The Gerontologist, 38* (4), 481-489.

+ Collins, N. L., Dunke-Schetter, C., Lobel, M., & Scrimshaw, S. C. M. (1993). Social support and pregnancy: Psychological correlates of birth outcomes and postpartum depression. *Journal of Personality and Social Psychology, 65*, 1243-1258.

+ Compton, W. & Hoffman, E. (2013). *Positive psychology : the science of happiness and flourishing*. Belmont, CA: Wadsworth Cengage Learning.

+ Cousins, N. (1981). Anatomy of an illness as perceived by the patient: Reflections on healing and regeneration. Toronto New York: Bantam Books.

+ Cowlishaw, S., Niele, S., Teshuva, K., Browning, C., & Kendig, H. (2013). Older adults'
spirituality and life satisfaction: a longitudinal test of social support and sense of
coherence as mediating mechanisms. Ageing and Society, 33, pp 1243-1262.

+ Dissanayake, M. P., & McConatha, J. T., (2011). Self identity and cultural context: A
comparative investigation of the self image and identity of Sri Lankans. World Cultures
eJournal, 18(2), 1-18.

+ "Family Economics and Nutrition Review". (1999). Poverty among women 11(1), 71-74.

+ Fleck, J. R. (1981). Dimensions of personal religion: A response to J. R. Fleck & J. D. Carter
(Eds.), Psychology and Christianity, 66-80. New York: Harper Row.

+ Fontane, P.E. (1996). Exercise, fitness, and feeling well. American Behavioral Scientist,
39, 288-305.

+ Fowler, J. W. (1981). Stages of faith. San Francisco: Harper & Row.

+ Fredrickson, B. L. (2001). The role of positive emotions in positive psychology: The
Broaden-and-Build theory of positive emotions. American Psychologist, 56(3), 218-226.

+ Gallup, G. H. (1987). The Gallup poll: Public opinion 1986. Wilmington, DE: Scholarly
Resources.

+ Gartner, J., Larson, D. B., & Allen, G. D. (1991). Religious commitment and mental health:
A review of the empirical literature. Journal of Psychology & Theology, 19, 6-25.

+ Genia, V. & Shaw, D. G. (1991). Religion, Intrinsic extrinsic orientation and depression.
Review of Religious Research, 32, 274-283.

+ Gorsuch, R. L. (1988). Psychology of religion. Annual Review of Psychology, 39, 201–221.

+ Green, L. W. & Ottoson, J. M. (1999). Community and population health. (pp. 44). (8th
Ed.). New York: McGraw-Hill Companies, Inc.

+ Grossman, L. K. (1998). Aging viewers: The best is yet to come. Columbia Journalism
Review, 36 (5), 568-569.

+ Guttmann, A. (2003). Identity in democracy. Princeton: Princeton University Press.

+ Helm, H. M., Hays, J. C., Flint, E. P., Koenig, H. G., & Blazer, D. G. (2000). Does private
religious activity prolong survival? A six-year follow-up study of 3,851 older adults.
Journal of Gerontology, 55A, M400-M405.

+ Hill, R.D., (2005). Positive aging. New York: W. W. Norton.

+ Jones, F. (2003). Religious commitment in Canada, 1997 and 2000. Religious
Commitment Monograph No. 3. Ottawa: Christian Commitment Research Institute.

+ Kahoe, R. D. & Meadow, M. J. (1981). A developmental perspective on religious
orientation dimensions. Journal of Religion and Health, 20, 8-17.

+ Kang, S., Shaver, P. R., Sue, S., Min, K., & Jing, H. (2003). Cultural-specific patterns in the prediction of life satisfaction: Role of emotion, relationship quality, and self esteem. *Personality and Social Psychology Bulletin, 29*(12), 1596-1608.

+ Kirsch, I. S., Jungeblut, A., Jenkins, L., & Kolstad. (September 1993). National adult literacy survey. *Adult Literacy in America* (No. AE 1075-131 C.5). Harrisburg, PA: National Center for Education Statistics

+ Krause, N. (2005). God-mediated control and psychological well-being in late life. *Research on Aging, 27*, 136-164.

+ Kubzansky, L. D., Berkman, L. F., Glass, T. A., & Seeman, T. E. (1998). Is educational attainment associated with shared determinants of health in the elderly? Findings from the MacArthur studies of successful aging. *American Psychosomatic Society, 60*, 578-585.

+ Labouvie-Vief, G., & Medler, M. (2002). Affect optimization and affect complexity: Modes and styles of regulation in adulthood. *Psychology and Aging, 17*, 571-587.

+ Maltby, J., & Day, l. (2003). Religious orientation, religious coping and appraisals of stress: assessing primary appraisal factors in the relationship between religiosity and psychological well-being. *Personality and individual differences, 34* (7), 1209-1224.

+ McFadden, S. H. (1996). Religion, Spirituality, and aging. In J. E. Birren & K. W. Schaie (Eds.), *Handbook of the psychology of aging* (pp. 162-177). San Diego: Academic Press.

+ Nussbaum, K. & Michaux, W. (1963). Response to humor in depression: A predictor and evaluator of patient change? *Psychiatric Quarterly, 37* (3), 527-539.

+ Palmore, E. (2004). Research note: Ageism in Canada and the United States. *Journal of Cross-Cultural Gerontology 19*(1). 41-46.

+ Pennsylvania Interdepartmental Human Services Planning Committee. (1992). *PA County Planning Data Kit.* (Pub. 218- 10/92).

+ Philadelphia Health Management Corporation. (1997). *Regional Health Trend Analysis.* Customized for Chester County Health Department.

+ Princeton Religion Research Center. (1999). *Religious Practices in the United States.* Princeton, NJ: Author.

+ Richmond, L., (2011). "5 Spiritual practices for aging well". *Huffington Post.* Retrieved September 25, 2013 from http://www.huffingtonpost.com/lewis-richmond/five-spiritual-practices-aging-well_b_1165552.html

+ Santrock, J. W. (2004). *Life-span development* (9th Ed.). New York: McGraw-Hill.

+ Scott, E., (2013). "Maintain a sense of humor". *About.com.* Retrieved September 28, 2013 from http://stress.about.com/od/positiveattitude/ht/humor.htm.

+ Seligman, M.E.P., & Csikszentmihalyi, M. (2000). Positive psychology: An introduction. *American Psychologist, 55*, 5-14.

+ Schieman, S., Pudrovska, T., & Milkie, M. A. (2005). The sense of divine control and the self-concept: A study of race differences in late life. *Research on Aging, 27*, 165-196.

+ Stamler, J. (1998). Setting the TONE for ending the hypertension epidemic. *The Journal of the American Medical Association, 279* (11), 878-883.

+ Starks, S., & Hughey, A. W. (2003). African American Women at Midlife: The Relationship Between Spirituality and Life Satisfaction. *Affilia, 18* (2), 133-147.

+ Strawbridge, W. J., Shema, S. J., Cohen, R. D., & Kaplan, G. A. (2001). Religious attendance increases survival by improving and maintaining good health behaviors. *Annals of Behavioral Medicine, 23*, 68-74.

+ Thoresen, C. E., & Harris, A. H. S. (2002). Spirituality and health: What's the evidence and what's needed? *Annals of Behavioral Medicine, 24*, 3-13

+ U.S. Bureau of the Census. (1998). *Estimates of the Population of Counties by Age, Sex, Race, and Hispanic Origin: 1990-1997.* (No. P. 20-491). U.S. Bureau of the Census.

+ Ventis, W. L. (1995). The relationships between religion and mental health. *Journal of Social Issues, 51*, 33-48.

+ Wink, P., & Dillon, M. (2002). Spiritual development across the adult life course: Findings from a longitudinal study. *Journal of Adult Development, 9*, 79-94.

+ Wulff, D. M. (1997). *Religion: classic and contemporary* (Vol. 2). London: John Wiley & Sons.

CHAPTER SEVEN

The Healing Power of Nature

CHAPTER SEVEN

The Healing Power of Nature

Many of us spend our days in offices, under artificial lights, working on computers, in cubicles that have no windows. When we finally complete our workday and emerge, it is often dark and we have spent another day of our lives in an artificial environment with no access to sunlight, trees, flowers, beaches, or parks. Nature deprivation negatively impacts the health and happiness of people of all ages. Psychologists have associated an increase in stress-related illnesses, depression, and anxiety with our increasing alienation from nature.

A new form of therapy, eco therapy, focuses on the importance of time spent in the natural environment. This viewpoint stresses that people are wired to interact with air, water, plants, and other animals in order to be happy, thrive, and even to survive. Alienation from nature is as devastating for our health as alienation from social relationships. Natural environments are healing; they help us feel better, manage stress better, and gain perspective (Walsh, 2011).

A 2007 study in England found that a daily dose of walking outside could be as effective as taking antidepressant drugs for treating mild to moderate depression. A recent report from the BBC addressed the importance of parks, gardens, and green spaces in the promotion of health and happiness (Walsh, 2011). Report on the survey results of over 5,000 households, the study found that those individuals who live in greener areas were significantly healthier and happier.

THE HEALING POWER OF GARDENS

The notion that fresh air and a beautiful natural setting promote health and relaxation is not new. However social science is only recently beginning to incorporate the healing power of nature into research on health and well-being. In a study addressing the benefits of hospital gardens, Franklin (2012) focused on the promotion of relaxation and restoration from visits to tree–filled vistas,

fountains, greenery, and flowering plants. In other words, there is a healing power associated with "window views." According to Franklin, the following garden guidelines tend to promote healing:

1. Keep it green
2. Keep it interesting
3. Engage multiple senses
4. Mind the walkways
5. Water with care
6. Make entry easy

Healing gardens have existed in many cultures. The Persian garden for example was always considered a magical place for socializing, relaxation, spirituality and prayer — a paradise on earth. The beautiful garden in Isfahan is one example of a Persian garden. It is a peaceful place visited by thousands each year.

In fact the word "paradise" is derived from the Old Persian implying an enclosed garden. This term was adopted by the Christians as the Garden of Eden. Persian carpets are based on the notion of a Persian garden, with walls, fountains, and flowering shrubs along the perimeter. The fountains in the center present an important metaphor for calmness and reflection into one's soul, thus the garden is perceived as a place of spiritual reflection. Fountains at the center of gardens also provide a soothing background for meditation and reflection.

Researchers who have studied leisure, discussed in an earlier chapter, have focused on the importance of nature and gardens in promoting health and well-being. In fact Unruh and Hutchinson (2011) state that gardening may be particularly conducive to promoting enjoyment, relaxation, and even a spiritual experience. These researchers found that gardeners spoke of feeling close to nature and experiencing a bond with birds and animals as a result of being outside. The participants of Unruh and Hutchinson's study found that gardening was a means through which their participants connected with their inner life, renewed themselves, and coped with illness. They concluded that leisure time promoted a reappraisal of life situations and was useful as a coping mechanism.

Time spent in nature is like free therapy with no side effects. Interaction with nature also promotes increased cognitive functioning such as attention and memory (Berman, Jonides, & Kaplan, 2008). Time in nature has been shown to be renewing. Korpela and Kinnunen (2010) found that leisure time, time where participants of their study interacted with nature, helped in recovery from work demands. Time in nature served the purpose of promoting relaxation, recovery from stress, and improved life satisfaction.

HEALTH, NATURE, AND VITAMIN D

Vitamin D deficiency is becoming a serious health concern in the United States and other countries. There is a direct relationship between time in fresh air and sunshine and one's levels of vitamin D. Recent studies have indicated that there is a widespread problem with vitamin D deficiency in the United States. Vitamin D is known as the sunshine vitamin. It is produced in the body in response to sunlight and certain naturally occurring foods, such as fish, eggs, diary and grain products. Vitamin D is essential for strong bones and helps the body use necessary calcium. Given the concerns of osteoporosis and bone damage in later life, a vitamin D deficiency can prove to be a serious health threat. Vitamin D deficiency has been associated with increased risk of death from cardiovascular disease, cognitive impairment in older adults, and even breathing problems such as asthma and an increased risk of certain cancers.

Vitamin D can help prevent or treat diabetes and hypertension as well as bone and muscle weakness. Although a number of causes can lead to vitamin D deficiency, getting outside in natural sunlight can prevent a vitamin D deficiency in many older men and women.

TIME IN NATURE AND OPTIMISM

Spending time in nature, in the sunshine, taking a walk, a bike ride, a hike, a boat ride, will reduce stress and promote optimism about life, a more positive outlook when coping with negative life events. Sitting on a beach enjoying the view of the water, perhaps watching dolphins swim by reduces stress and leads to increased happiness. This free and natural healing is referred to as ecotherapy. Ecotherapy is a new and promising field in psychology. It promotes well-being by focusing on the beneficial relationship derived from time in nature. Howard Clinebell (1996), the first to use the term, defined ecotherapy as healing and growth nurtured by a healthy interaction with the earth. Nature has been shown to promote faster healing after surgery, to reduce pain, and to keep illness at bay. It even helps people recover from depression

In the 20 years that I have worked with older adults studying ways of promoting well-being and happiness, I have never found a single instance where someone did not feel better after taking time out and spending time in nature. Given the numerous benefits that can be derived from gardens, beaches, parks, mountains, lakes, even patios, it is surprising that there is not more emphasis placed on ecotherapy as an inexpensive and effective way of helping people cope with stress.

SMALL CHANGES MAKE A BIG DIFFERENCE

Studies exploring the relationship between stress and aging have asked people: What keeps you going? What helps you cope? Most people respond that it is a positive attitude, such as optimism, a sense of enjoying life, perseverance with life goals, spirituality, satisfying relationships, and active engagement (Atchley, 1999). One crucial way of integrating many of these coping strategies is to take time in nature, to walk, to run, to sit in the sun, to appreciate the beauty of nature. The healing power of nature should not be underestimated. As Melinda's example illustrates, even relatively short periods of time outside can have numerous positive benefits.

Melinda is in her late 60s. She has recently retired and is teaching English to immigrants on a part-time basis. Melinda has always experienced considerable anxiety and has difficulty sleeping. After she retired, she decided that she would spend one half-hour to one hour a day walking in a nearby park. This hour has become her relaxation and meditative time. She thinks about her life as she walks; she enjoys the trees and shrubs she sees along the way. She occasionally chats with people she meets on her walks. This small change in her life, one-half to one hour most days, has transformed her life. She feels better, she is more fit, has lost 8 pounds, and most of all, she feels calmer and happier. For the first time in years, she is even sleeping through the night. Melinda wonders why she did not make this simple change in her life earlier.

PAY ATTENTION: MINDLESSNESS AND MINDFULNESS

We are often not aware or even psychologically present in our life experiences. We often eat, talk, drive, walk, and even have sex without fully experiencing the moment. We frequently lose awareness of what is going on in our lives. In our complex and technologically saturated world, mindlessness is becoming more and more common. We tend to multitask, simultaneously checking text messages and emails as we talk on the phone and listen to music. As a consequence, we often do not fully attend to any of the things we are doing.

Mindfulness is a new and very popular way of refocusing our attention on our lives. It is a useful coping mechanism. Being present is the first step to take in the struggle to cope with the concerns in our lives. Mindfulness involves making an effort to be present in our life experiences. Jon Kabat-Zinn (2005), one of the founders of the contemporary Mindfulness-Based Stress Reduction movement, defines mindfulness as paying non-judgmental attention to the present moment. From this perspective, mindfulness compels us to focus squarely on our routine activities.

I try to avoid eating at my desk. Yesterday, I had a long day. As a consequence, I brought a lunch and a dinner to eat at work. I had planned to go outside, sit in the lovely fall weather, take a break, and eat lunch. Just as I was leaving the office, a friend called with a problem. Hungry, I sat down and started to eat. When I had completed my phone conversation 15 minutes later, I looked down and realized that I had eaten not only my lunch sandwich but also all the vegetables and chips and cookies I had brought for my dinner. I had not only consumed a large amount of food I did not plan to eat, but I had done so without a modicum of pleasure. I had not paid attention. I had not been present and in the moment.

We all have had similar experiences. Time passes by in a flash, and we are unaware of what has just occurred. In order to participate in our lives, it is important to minimize these blackouts. Our life is made up of many moment-to-moment experiences. In order to live fully, we need to be aware of those experiences. Indeed, the experience of flow and the presence of spirituality, which were discussed in other chapters, are related to mindfulness.

Perspectives on the benefits of mindfulness vary. The ideas, of course, are not new. They have long been present in Eastern religious and philosophical traditions. They have become increasingly relevant, however, in our fast-paced world. In a world of multitasking, most of us rarely live in the present moment. We eat while we watch TV or read. We text as we watch TV. We talk on the phone as we cook. We send incessant text messages or read Facebook at home at social gatherings or in restaurants. As a professor, I have to endlessly remind my students that they need to pay attention in class. It is not OK to text or surf the Web when they are sitting in my classes.

The benefits of "mindful" practices have long been recognized by nearly every religious tradition. Even though they date back thousands of years, American psychologists have only recently begun to focus on the impact of mindfulness on psychological well-being. Jon Kabat-Zinn has adapted Eastern practices of mediation to develop mindfulness in contemporary society. Kabat-Zinn and others have developed an 8-week mindfulness training program that is focused on stress reduction. This program has been proven to be very successful in variety of situations (Snyder, Lopez, & Pedrotti, 2011). Therapists have recently begun to incorporate mindfulness into their treatment plans with considerable success.

The new focus on mindfulness, which has been called the "third wave" in psychological practice, has compelled therapists to help their clients develop skills that can teach them to be present in their day-to-day, moment-to-moment experiences. It is not easy to be present in the moment, however. In her books, Mindfulness (1989) and Counterclockwise (2009), Ellen Langer says that mindfulness involves a flexible state of mind, one that is actively engaged in the present. Langer goes on to suggest that by being more mindful we live more fully in the present, we are not being rigid and oblivious to alternative ways of knowing (Langer, 1989, 2009). No matter one's stage in life, being mindful in our lives, our relationships, or our work is a positive step. Because life is limited, we should live it fully.

IMPORTANT POINTS ON MINDFULNESS (SHAPIRO, SCHWARTZ, & SANTERRE, 2002)

1. Being non-judgmental
2. Being accepting
3. Developing patience
4. Being trusting
5. Being open
6. Being gentle
7. Being generous
8. Being empathetic
9. Showing gratitude
10. Being loving and kind
11. Letting go

The above points illustrate the psychological impact of being mindful. Clearly developing mindfulness and living our lives in a state of awareness has many positive consequences. How can we start? Many of us are too busy and stressed to begin the process.

Eastern philosophical views of mindfulness tend to focus on the relationship between mindfulness and ethical concentration and wisdom. Buddhist beliefs also discuss mindfulness as only one part of the Noble Eightfold Path:

1. Right speech
2. Right action
3. Right livelihood
4. Right effort
5. Right mindfulness
6. Right concentration
7. Right understanding
8. Right thought (de Silva, 1992)

Below are quick points taken from Charles Knoles (2013) article entitled "5 mini mindfulness methods that you can do anywhere". There are many such short tutorials available on line. There are also 8-week courses available at various mindfulness based programs and institutes around the world.

Five quick steps to being more mindful:
1. Meditate for 5 minutes — Sit down, close your eyes, and focus on something like your breath, an image, or a word —"one" is a popular choice — and simply allow your mind to drift, returning to your focus when you need to.
2. Breathe — This is easier said than done, slowing your breath calms you down.
3. Harness the Hand-Mind Connection — Stress notifies your body that you're in a dangerous situation. As a calming practice, try immersing your hands in warm water (rubbing them briskly together also works in a pinch) to open up the blood.
4. Un-tunnel Your Vision—Extend your arms to your side in a T-formation and wiggle your fingers. Then slowly bring your arms forward until the fingers are in sight, and then extend them out again. Repeat.
5. Tune in and Tune out—Charlie Knoles says to decrease your exposure to noisy environments. If that's not possible as you roam the city, wear ear buds — nobody will know they aren't plugged into your iPod!

Similar to spending time outside, increasing mindfulness is free and can exponentially improve happiness and life satisfaction. It can help us to slow down and savor the moments of our life. In our chaotic world, mindfulness serves as positive a powerful coping mechanism.

MANAGE STRESS AND INCREASE LIFE SATISFACTION AND HAPPINESS

We all strive to be happy, which is linked to a sense of life satisfaction. Life satisfaction involves an attempt to evaluate our past, our present and our thoughts about the future. Diener (1984) and Krause (1990) describe two theoretical approaches to the study of life satisfaction. The first approach is viewing satisfaction globally; the second approach explores the domains that shape life satisfaction. Those domains have been presented in this book —relationships, health, work, and income. These competing approaches to life satisfaction are also called "the bottom-up and top-down theories" (Diener, 1984, p. 565).

Put another way, can we say that our life satisfaction is dependent on a global perspective or is it the day-to-day aspects of our life, our relationships, our health, and our work that shape our life satisfaction. There is no clear answer to this question.

YOUR ENVIRONMENT IS IMPORTANT

The person-environmental fit model explains that in order to optimally manage our lives we need to live in spaces that "fit" our personality, lifestyle and interests. This is not always possible, but it is important for us to know that our capacity to manage stress is also connected to the spaces and places of our life —our neighborhood, community, city, and country. The person-environmental fit model (Kahana, 1982) focuses on the importance of an individual's "fit" between his or her abilities, lifestyle, plans and goals and the physical and social environment in which the person lives. It is important to have a balance between our various interests and competencies and the demands of our environment.

In later life, our well-being and our happiness are largely dependent upon the balance between who we are and demands, support and resources available to us in our environment. If our environment is too compensating, in other words, if it poses no challenges, no opportunities for growth, creativity, or for learning then it can lead to a decline in our capacities and decrease our well-being.

On the other hand, if our environment is too stressful or too challenging, if all of our personal and social resources are needed to cope with the demands of our environment, then the environment damages our lives. Healthy and positive adaptation results when the environmental press slightly exceeds our competence levels (Lawton, 1985). The environmental press can be managed by either altering the situational context (e.g., being placed in a situation where fewer demands are made on the individual) or by increasing individual competencies and stress management skills.

CONCLUDING THOUGHTS

The difference between a successful and unsuccessful aging experience depends on whether people are able to successfully manage difficult and stressful events in their life. Managing stress goes beyond coping with problems; it focuses on the promotion of happiness and well-being across the lifespan. Maintaining well-being is not easy; with age it can become even more challenging. The interactive influences of our habits, health practices, lifestyle choices, and personal and environmental stressors have a cumulative influence on our well-being. Numerous studies have found that health-promoting behaviors and lifestyles affect the mortality rates precipitated by heart disease, various cancers, cerebrovascular disease, pneumonia and influenza, and diabetes — the leading causes of death in older adults. One of the top factors influencing lifestyle is our perception of the stress in our lives and our appraisal of the resources we have available to us to cope with the stressors we experience.

Unmanageable stress can threaten health and well-being in later adulthood (Tahmaseb McConatha & Volkwein-Kaplan, 2012). The information reviewed in this book notes that a person's subjective feelings of well-being are influenced by a number of variables: perception of control and competence, satisfaction with social and emotional relationships, life satisfaction, and subjective health.

As people grow older, there are many changes. Some are positive and some are negative. Life is comprised of a series of gains and losses. This book has explored how to cope with later life threats and challenges. The key to successful aging is to accept and adapt to age-related changes by developing and/or maintaining healthy behaviors and lifestyles. Older adults who utilize effective coping strategies, rely on their support systems, and remain cognitively, physically, and socially active. They are more likely to avoid a decline in their physical and mental abilities.

Healthy lifestyles can increase independence and promote overall life satisfaction for a significantly longer period of time. Stress management programs need to increase older adults' awareness that one of the consequences of unhealthily behaviors and lifestyles can result in decline.

There are realities associated with aging — physical decline, an increase in vulnerability to illness, loss of social roles, and loss of loved ones. However all of the research indicates that despite stressful life events, later life can be a happy and satisfying time of life. Most people are able to adapt to age-related changes without loss of self-esteem and happiness. There is no one way to successfully adapt to any stage of life. Evaluations of life are objective and subjective, individual and communal; there are many pathways to successful aging. Havighurst, Neugarten, and Tobin (1963) were some of the first researchers to evaluate life satisfaction in late life. They proposed five components of life satisfaction that are still relevant today.

1. Zest for life
2. Resolution and fortitude — not giving up easily, making the most of life, taking the good with the bad.
3. Completion — feeling that one has made a contribution in life, that one has accomplished what one hoped to.
4. Self-esteem — it is important to feel good about oneself, to feel that one has value and worth.
5. A positive outlook or optimism in life.

Older adults are as satisfied and happy as younger adults. Happiness and life satisfaction can be obtained regardless of age.

REFERENCES

+ Atchley, R. (1999). *Continuity and adaptation in aging : creating positive experiences.*
Baltimore, Md: Johns Hopkins University Press.

+ Berman, M.G., Jonides, J., & Kaplan, S. (2008). The cognitive benefits of interacting with
nature. *Psychological Science, 19,* 1207–1212.

+ Clinebell, H. (1996). *Ecotherapy: Healing Ourselves, Healing the Earth.* Minneapolis, MN:
Fortress Press.

+ de Silva, Lynn A. (1992). „Dialogue in the Context of Sri Lanka Buddhism", in Francis,
T. Dayananda and Balasundaram, F. J., *Asian expressions of Christian commitment: a
reader in Asian theology* (pp. 394–406.). Madras: Christian Literature Society.

+ Diener, E. (1984). Subjective well-being. *Psychological Bulletin, 95,* 542-575.

+ Franklin, D. (2011). "How hospital gardens help patients' head." *Scientific American.*
Retrieved August 13, 2013 from http://www.scientificamerican.com/article.
cfm?id=nature-that-nurtures

+ Havighurst, R. J., Neugarten, B. L., & Tobin, S. S. (1963). Disengagement, personality and
life satisfaction in the later years. In P. F. Hansen (Ed.), *Age with a future* (pp. 419-425).
Copenhagen: Munksgaard.

+ Kabat-Zinn, J. (2005). *Wherever you go, there you are: mindfulness meditation in
everyday life.* New York, N.Y: Hyperion.

+ Kahana, E. (1982). A congruence model of person-environment interaction. In M. P.
Lawton, P.G. Windley, & T. O. Byerts (Eds.), *Aging and the Environment: Theoretical
Approaches* (pp. 97-121). New York: Springer.

+ Knoles, C. (2013). "5 mini mindfulness methods that you can do anywhere". *Well+Good
NYC.* Retrieved August 17, 2013 from http://www.wellandgoodnyc.com/2013/02/12/5-
mini-mindfulness-methods-that-you-can-do-anywhere/#

+ Korpela, K & Kinnunen, U. (2010). How is leisure time interacting with nature related to
the Need for recovery from work demands? Testing multiple mediators. *Leisure Sciences
33*(1). 1-14.

+ Krause, N. (1990). Stressful events and life satisfaction among elderly men and women.
Journal of Gerontology 46(2). S84-S92.

+ Langer, E. (1989). *Mindfulness.* Reading, Mass: Perseus Books.

+ Langer, E. (2009). *Counterclockwise : Mindful Health and the Power of Possibility.* New
York: Ballantine Books.

+ Lawton, M.P. (1985). The elderly in context: Perspectives from environmental psychology and gerontology. *Environment and Behavior, 17*, 501-519.

+ Shapiro, S. L., Schwartz, G. E., & Santerre, C. (2002). Meditation and Positive Psychology. In C.R. Snyder and S. Lopez (Eds.), *Handbook of Positive Psychology*, (pp. 632–645). Oxford, UK: Oxford University Press.

+ Snyder, C., Lopez, S. & Pedrotti, J. (2011). *Positive Psychology: The Scientific and Practical Explorations of Human Strengths*. Thousand Oaks, CA: SAGE.

+ Tahmaseb-McConatha, J & K. Volkwein-Caplan. (2012) *The Social Geography of Healthy Aging*. Oxford, England: Meyer&Meyer.

+ Unruh, A. & Hutchinson, S. (2011). Embedded spirituality: Gardening in daily life and stressful life experiences. *Sc and J Caring Science 25*(3). 567-74.

+ Walsh, B. (2009). "'Eco-therapy' for environmental depression." *Time*. Retrieved September 13, 2013 from http://content.time.com/time/health/article/0,8599,1912687,00.html.

PICTURE CREDITS

Layout & Typesetting: Cornelia Knorr

Copy-editing: Michelle Demeter